THE
VENISON
COOKBOOK

Jim and Lois Zumbo

THE VENISON COOKBOOK

More than 200
Tested Recipes for
Deer, Elk,
Moose, and
Other Game

Prentice Hall Press • New York

Published by Prentice Hall Press
A Division of Simon & Schuster, Inc.

PRENTICE HALL PRESS is a trademark of Simon & Schuster, Inc.

LC No. 86-60063

ISBN: 0-13-941519-X

Manufactured in the United States of America
Designed by Alice R. Mauro

10 9 8 7 6 5 4 3 2 1

*T*o our children—Janette, Dan, Judi, and Angela—
our venison tasters and testers,
who have participated in many of our hunts
and have cheerfully, and sometimes
not so cheerfully, partaken of hundreds of
venison meals over the years.

Contents

We hope you'll enjoy our many delightful venison dishes, and if you follow our recipes, which we've enjoyed collecting and testing, you should have no problem producing an epicurean repast. Generous second helpings will be the rule at your table, if you do your part right in the kitchen, and we're betting you'll have very few scraps left over for the family canine.

Enjoy.

Jim and Lois Zumbo

Venison:
From Woods
to Freezer

So your venison is down! You've made a good shot, and the hunt is over. In front of you lies a large animal that somehow must be transported out of the woods and, ultimately, to your freezer.

The size of the animal determines the amount of calories and perspiration you'll expend getting it out of the woods. If you've downed a 40-pound whitetail in South Carolina, you will probably carry it out easily. But if you've toppled a 1,000-pound bull elk high on a Wyoming ridgetop, you have a major project on your hands.

For the most part, however, the average quarry will be a deer-sized animal. Generally, a fawn will field dress from 50 to 75 pounds, a yearling buck or doe about 80 to 120 pounds, an adult doe from 120 to 150 pounds, and a big buck from 150 to 200 pounds or more. First, we'll discuss the problem of getting a deer out of the woods, and then we'll tackle the logistics of transporting big animals such as elk, moose, and the like.

After you properly tag and field dress the deer, you must consider two factors—how far you have to move the carcass and your physical condition. If the animal is small, the terrain is level, and you're in reasonably good shape, you shouldn't have a problem. But, if you aren't in good condition, get help from your buddies or other hunters, regardless of the situation. The extra exertion of moving an animal might cause a serious problem. Don't take chances.

If you're up to the task of transporting the deer, the standard means is to drag it out. Before dragging the deer, do some advance planning first. Look over the area you have to travel with the deer. Consider the steepness of the terrain, the amount of underbrush, and the distance from the animal to the destination. Also, keep in mind that if you drag the deer you'll damage the hide. Never attempt to drag the carcass if you intend to have the head mounted because you might ruin the cape. Walk a proposed route to see if it will minimize efforts. Try a number of possibilities to find the easiest. Of course, sometimes there is no easy way. If you killed your deer in a hollow or in the bottom of a canyon, you might have no choice but to go up—and "up" means trouble.

Be cautious if you attempt a strenuous drag. All sorts of things can happen to your anatomy. You can hurt your back, pull a muscle, or even worse. When traveling uphill, you're pulling hard and using some forgotten muscles that will protest. If the undergrowth is thick, you'll have even more difficulty. Every root, twig, and particle of brush will snag you and the carcass while you're dragging. If there's snow on the ground, you'll have an easier time because the deer will slide along with less friction.

There are things you can do to help in dragging. Instead of grabbing the deer and pulling, lift its head off the ground as high as possible. Tie a rope around the antler bases and make a loop a short distance away for a handhold. If the animal is a doe, tie the rope around the neck just under the chin. If the animal is a buck, you can also tie a sturdy stick across the antlers and use the stick as a handle.

It's always a good idea to tie the front feet of the deer up around the back of the head. That keeps them from snagging on brush and getting in the way. You can also simply cut the legs off at the knee joints before making the drag.

Wear gloves when you drag a deer, regardless of the air temperature. They'll prevent your fingers from getting sore, and you'll have a better grip. Switch hands as often as necessary.

Be extra careful if you're dragging a buck. His antlers are sharply pointed, and they'll cause you plenty of grief and pain if you accidentally stumble into them. If you're dragging a deer downhill, be wary of its momentum carrying it along too rapidly. The carcass could overtake you and cause injury if you're in the way.

Never drag a deer backwards. Always pull it along with the grain of the pelt—in other words, head first.

If you decide not to drag the deer, you can cut the carcass into pieces and carry the meat out in chunks, or you might try piggybacking the carcass on your shoulders, if the deer is small enough and you're big enough. A word of warning—if you carry the carcass on your back, make sure you decorate the animal so that it doesn't look like a deer. You could be mistaken for a live deer by another hunter. Drape plenty of orange ribbon on the animal, if you have some, or cover it with an orange vest.

Boning the carcass in the woods and carrying out only the edible meat will save you plenty of weight. That is a good option if you've dropped a deer in a remote region, such as mule deer country in the western mountains.

Here's what you'll be faced with if you kill a deer that field dresses around 115 pounds and you decide to bone the carcass in the woods. According to a study, the head weighs 8½ pounds, the hide is 9½ pounds, the meat trimmed from a typical bullet wound and the fat will weigh 25 pounds, and the bones will weigh 11 pounds. By discarding this material in the woods, you leave behind 54 pounds for the foxes and coyotes, and you carry out only 61 pounds.

You'll need certain equipment to bone a carcass in the woods. A knife with a long, flexible blade is ideal, and you should have a sharpening stone to touch up the kinfe as it dulls. A generous supply of cheesecloth is necessary to wrap the meat in, and a large rucksack or backpack is required to carry the wrapped venison.

If you don't want to go through the chore of boning the carcass, you can cut it in halves or quarters and take out the sections on a packboard. If the deer is large and dresses out at 125 pounds or better, you might be able to haul it out in two trips, if you're sturdy and have a strong back. If not, make an extra trip or two to avoid seeing a surgeon or chiropractor about a hernia or backache.

If you're hunting small deer, you can cut off the legs and stuff the carcass into a large rucksack.

Whatever method you decide to use to get your deer out of the woods, be absolutely sure you're familiar with the laws in your state concerning the evidence of the sex of the carcass. In some states you might not be allowed to sever the head from the animal or remove the testicles.

Another way to haul out a deer is to lash the animal to a pole and carry it out with a hunter at each end. That technique is not as easy as it sounds. First, you must locate a pole that will support the weight of a deer, but one that is not so heavy that it will be impossible to lift. Also, the deer will sway from side to side as it is carried, throwing the carriers off balance. The best way to prevent swaying is to securely lash the head to the pole. Put some kind of protection on your shoulders where the pole rests since they will quickly become sore without it. A hunting vest or extra piece of apparel will suffice.

If you're an enterprising soul, you can rig up a travois to haul out your deer, as the Indians often did. That requires some time and material to put it together and is seldom used by hunters. However, if constructed properly, it is a rather nice vehicle to transport the carcass.

In some areas, especially the West, hunters use one-wheeled carts to haul deer. They are usually homemade devices constructed with lightweight metal tubing and a bicycle wheel. A few commercial companies now make such vehicles. If you down a deer in "no man's land," a cart is a valuable piece of equipment. We've seen them transport deer out of really rough country.

If you're prepared, you can carry out a deer on a litter or stretcher. Lash or roll an old sheet of canvas or blanket between two poles, but be sure the material is securely fastened or the weight of the carcass will collapse it.

A horse makes an excellent vehicle to haul out your deer, but most hunters don't own horses. Western outfitters commonly employ them, because mule-deer country is so vast and rugged that a sturdy steed is often the only way to transport a carcass. If you're not familiar with horses and find yourself in a situation where one is available, never attempt to load a deer without expert advice. There's much more to it than simply tossing a deer over a horse's back. You can hurt yourself or the horse if you don't know what you're doing.

The very best way to haul out a deer is, of course, to drop

your quarry next to a road. Then you can drive up, grab a leg, and swing the carcass up into your vehicle. How nice it would be if that happened every time, but that's rarely the case. As the old saying goes, the fun of the hunt ends when you pull the trigger. How true.

If you're after bigger game than deer, such as elk or moose, you usually have to section the carcass to get it out, although there are times when you can drive up to the animal and load it in one piece. But you'll need plenty of help to do that.

Cutting a large animal into pieces is a big project. You must be prepared. Basic cutting tools include a good knife with a sturdy edge, a sharpening stone, a saw, and a belt ax or hatchet. You can carry those items on your belt, and many compact models are made for hunting purposes. In your daypack, which you should always carry on your back, put plenty of strong rope, a small block and tackle, and enough cheesecloth or meat sacks to accommodate the quarters.

Your first job will be to skin the animal. That chore can be done while the animal is lying on the ground.

Once the quarters are sectioned, hang them in the shade. This should be done if you plan to leave them and return later to haul them out. If the air temperature is warm, you'll probably have to contend with flies, which will quickly discover your animal. You can discourage them by sprinkling generous amounts of pepper on the carcass, but the most effective way is to completely cover the meat with cloth. If you suspect flies have had access to the meat, carefully check the carcass for egg clusters. If you catch them in time you can scrape them away. If maggots have already begun to work on the meat, cut away the affected part; then check the carcass even more closely. More maggots might be present.

If you must leave the carcass overnight, various creatures might help themselves to it. Foxes, coyotes, and birds will quickly move in unless you take precautions. Hang the meat high enough in a tree so it won't dangle close to the ground and within reach of four-footed animals. Birds can be discouraged by wrapping the meat in a cloth or game bag. If black bears are a threat, hang the carcass from a springy limb several feet away from the trunk of the tree and as high as possible.

Beware of human thieves as well. Unfortunately, some people will help themselves to your animal, if they think they can get away with it. Use your judgment before leaving the carcass behind—it may be wise to conceal it.

Regardless of how you get the meat out of the woods, always remember one word—cool. Keep the carcass as cool as possible every step of the way. That's one of the most important aspects of quality venison. If you don't take care of the meat from the moment it hits the ground, you'll have regrets at the dinner table.

Once you've gotten the carcass or quarters to a vehicle or camp, then what? Let's look at the options.

The easiest thing is to load up the deer, drive a short distance to your house or meat processor, and take it from there. But, if you have a long distance to travel, you'll need to pay attention to a number of details.

If you plan to haul the meat home in a vehicle, you can take it to a processor who will cut up the carcass, quick-freeze it, and pack it for transportation. Be sure the deer is aged properly before it's cut up.

During the peak period of deer season, don't count on quick service from the processor. You'll probably have to wait in a long line.

In the event that you want to take the carcass home in one piece, be sure it's thoroughly chilled before wrapping it. An old sleeping bag or quilt makes a good cover. Wrap the animal tightly, and you'll be pleasantly surprised how long it will stay cold. Three or four days is not an unusual length of time, even during hot weather. Never wrap the meat in plastic, since plastic doesn't breathe and can trap heat. When traveling, place the meat in the vehicle away from the windows so the sun doesn't shine on it. If you have a two- or three-day drive and the nights are crispy cool, unwrap the meat at night so it will chill. Wrap it again in the morning before driving on.

If you're flying, it's no problem to transport meat on the aircraft. For best results, freeze or chill the meat immediately before departure, wrap the meat tightly in several layers of freezer paper, and check it as baggage. Arrange flights so there are as few layovers or plane changes as possible. If your trip is an extended one, ship dry ice with the meat, but make sure you fill out the proper airline forms.

Another option is to leave the meat with a processor and have him ship the meat to your home. That can be an expensive proposition, but well worth it if you like venison.

It's also possible in many areas to trade the meat to a processor in return for venison sausage and salami and other types of meats. All you do is weigh the meat and exchange it for an equal amount of already processed venison. You'll have to pay for the processed meat you obtain, and the price varies with the type of venison.

Take good care of your venison. You'll be rewarded at dinner time. The recipes in this book will guide you through many marvelous meals, but it's up to you to bring home a good piece of meat.

SOUPS
AND SAUCES AS
INGREDIENTS

*Several recipes in this book call for
the use of soups and sauces. If you'd like
to prepare your own, rather than use
a can from the store shelf, try your hand at these.
The ingredients are readily available from
any well-stocked grocery market.*

Cream of Chicken Soup

---

1 5-lb. stewing chicken, cut up
10 cups water
¼ cup chopped celery
¼ cup chopped onion
1 bay leaf
1 tablespoon salt
¼ cup chopped parsley
Butter
Flour

Place chicken, water, celery, onion, bay leaf, salt, and parsley in a large kettle. Simmer for 3 hours or until chicken is tender. Remove chicken and debone. Measure chicken stock and return stock and deboned chicken to pot. Using 1 tablespoon butter and 1 tablespoon flour for each cup of stock in the pot, make thickening sauce as follows. Melt butter in a saucepan. Add flour gradually, mixing well. Then add 2 cups stock a little at a time, stirring constantly. Bring to a boil, then cook for 5 minutes. Returned thickened mixture to the rest of the stock and the chicken and simmer 5 minutes longer.

Cream of Celery Soup

4 cups celery with leaves, cut small
4 cups water
2 teaspoons salt
Milk or cream
½ cup butter
½ cup flour

Combine celery, water, and salt. Simmer for 1 hour or until tender. Cool slightly. Puree in a blender, adding enough milk or cream to make 4 cups. Melt butter in saucepan. Stir in flour. Pour in celery-milk mixture slowly. Bring to a boil, stirring constantly.

Cream of Mushroom Soup

2 tablespoons butter or margarine
1 cup (about ¼ pound) sliced whole
  mushrooms
2 tablespoons chopped onion
2 tablespoons flour
2 cups chicken broth
½ cup light cream
½ teaspoon salt
¼ teaspoon pepper
¼ teaspoon nutmeg

In a Dutch oven, melt butter and saute mushrooms and onions for 5 minutes. Add flour and blend. Add broth gradually, stirring constantly. Simmer about 5 minutes until thickened. Cool slightly. Add cream and seasonings. Heat through and serve or use immediately.

Tomato Soup

3½ cups canned tomatoes
1 small onion
1 bay leaf
1 tablespoon chopped
   parsley
¼ teaspoon baking soda
6 ounces tomato paste
¼ cup butter
¼ cup flour
2 cups milk
1½ tablespoons salt
1 tablespoon sugar

Simmer tomatoes, onion, bay leaf, and parsley in a large kettle for 10 minutes. Cool slightly. Puree in a blender. Add baking soda and tomato paste. Mix well. Melt butter in the kettle. Blend in flour. Add milk gradually, stirring constantly. Cook until thick and smooth, stirring constantly. Add salt. Add tomato mixture, a little at a time. Mix well and add sugar. Bring to a simmer and serve or use immediately.

Barbecue Sauce

¼ cup vinegar
½ cup water
2 teaspoons mustard
¾ teaspoon salt
⅛ teaspoon pepper
½ cup ketchup
½ teaspoon cayenne pepper
1 thick slice of lemon
1 slice onion, slivered
¼ cup margarine
1½ teaspoon liquid smoke

Combine all ingredients in a saucepan. Simmer 15 minutes.

Chili Sauce

---

1 medium onion, chopped
2 cloves garlic, chopped
½ cup oil
½ cup flour
1½ quarts hot chicken stock
½ cup tomato puree
7 ounches chili powder
Water
Salt to taste

Sauté onion and garlic in oil in saucepan. Add flour to make a thick paste. Add hot chicken stock, tomato puree, and salt. Simmer 10 to 15 minutes. Dissolve the chili powder in a small amount of water, and pour into the saucepan. Reduce heat to very low and simmer about 30 minutes. Strain and add salt to taste.

Taco Sauce

---

2 small cans hot green chilies, chopped
2 cups tomato sauce
3 teaspoons olive oil
3 teaspoons vinegar
1 teaspoon oregano
Dash of cumin powder
Salt to taste

Remove seeds and membranes from chilies. Combine all ingredients and mix thoroughly until blended.

Enchilada Sauce

---

4 medium tomatoes (1½ lbs.), or 15 ounces
   tomato puree
3 tablespoons chili powder
1 medium onion, chopped
1 clove garlic, minced
1 teaspoon salt
¼ teaspoon sugar
1 tablespoon cooking oil

If using fresh tomatoes, peel and core tomatoes. Cut into quarters and puree in blender. Measure 2 cups of fresh tomato puree or 15 ounces tomato puree into blender container. Add chili powder, onion, garlic, salt, and sugar. Blend until smooth. In 1½-quart saucepan, combine tomato mixture and cooking oil. Stir over medium heat about 10 minutes or until sauce is slightly thickened. Makes 2 cups.

Marinara Sauce

4 tablespoons olive oil
3 cloves garlic, sliced very thinly crosswise
46 ounces tomato juice
28 ounces tomato sauce
1/2 teaspoon oregano leaves
1/4 teaspoon basil leaves
1/3 teaspoon garlic salt

In a Dutch oven, brown garlic slices in olive oil until very brown. Remove from heat. Remove garlic from the oil. When the oil is cool enough to prevent spattering, pour tomato juice and tomato sauce into oil. Return to a moderately high burner and add oregano, basil, and garlic salt. Simmer 2½ hours, stirring occasionally. Makes 1 quart.

Guacamole

---

2 medium avocados, peeled, pitted,
    and mashed
2 medium tomatoes, peeled, cored,
    and mashed
1 small onion, grated
2 tablespoons chili powder
1 tablespoon olive oil
2 teaspoons lime juice
2 teaspoon lemon juice
⅛ teaspoon paprika
¼ teaspoon pepper
¼ teaspoon coriander

Mix avocados, tomatoes, and onion together. Add other ingredients and mix very well.

SOUPS
AND STEWS

Venison Soup

2 pounds ground venison
¾ cup diced onion
4 tablespoons cooking oil
1 clove garlic, minced
1½ cup diced potatoes
1 cup diced carrots
½ cup barley
1 cup beef bouillon
½ teaspoon thyme
2 bay leaves
1½ teaspoons salt
¼ teaspoon pepper
2 to 2½ quarts water
29 ounces canned whole tomatoes
    (2½ cups)

Brown meat and onion in oil in a Dutch oven until onions are soft and meat loses its pink color. Add garlic, potatoes, carrots, barley, beef bouillon, thyme, bay leaves, salt, pepper, water, and tomatoes. Cover and simmer for 1½ to 2 hours. Add more water if necessary. Skim off any excess fat just before serving. Serves 6 to 8.

Utah High Country Stew

2 sliced onions
2 chopped green peppers
1 cup diced celery
3 tablespoons shortening
2 pounds venison stew meat, diced
½ teaspoon garlic salt or 1 minced garlic
    clove, plus ¼ teaspoon salt
¾ teaspoon salt
16 ounces tomato sauce
1 bay leaf
2 tablespoons picante sauce (optional)
2 cups water
3 diced potatoes
1 small turnip, diced
6 chopped carrots
¼ cup water and 3 tablespoons flour, mixed
    into a smooth paste

Sauté onions, peppers, and celery in shortening. Add meat, garlic salt, and salt. Brown meat on all sides, stirring frequently. Add tomato sauce, bay leaf, picante sauce, and water. Simmer 3 to 4 hours. Add potatoes, turnip, and carrots. Thicken to desired consistency with flour and water paste. Simmer 1 hour, adding more water if necessary, or until vegetables are tender. Serves 5 to 8.

Venison Microwave Minestrone

5 cups water
1 pound venison (any cut), cubed
1 small onion, diced
¼ teaspoon pepper
½ teaspoon leaf basil
½ cup diced carrots
16 ounces canned whole tomatoes
    (2 cups)
½ cup uncooked spaghetti, broken
    into 1-inch long pieces
2 medium zucchini (3 to 4 inches
    long), sliced unpeeled
16 ounces canned kidney beans,
    drained
1 cup green cabbage, finely shredded
1 teaspoon salt
Parmesan or Romano cheese, grated

In a 4-quart casserole suitable for a microwave, pour water over meat. Add onion, pepper, and basil. Cover, cook on HIGH in microwave for 25 to 35 minutes or until meat is tender, turning meat a couple of times. Add carrots and tomatoes. Cover and cook on HIGH for 10 minutes. Stir in spaghetti, zucchini, beans, cabbage, and salt. Cover and cook on HIGH for another 10 minutes, stirring once. Remove from oven and let stand 5 minutes. Serve each bowlful topped with grated cheese. Serves 6.

Stick-to-the-Ribs Stew

3 strips bacon, cut into small
    pieces
2 medium onions, diced
2 stalks celery, diced
1 diced green pepper
1 tablespoon cooking oil
2 pounds venison, cubed
½ teaspoon garlic salt
¼ teaspoon seasoned salt
½ teaspoon salt
⅛ teaspoon pepper
1½ quarts water
3 medium potatoes, diced
4 chopped carrots
1 diced rutabaga
10¾ ounces condensed cream
    of mushroom soup
2 tablespoons flour
4 to 5 tablespoons water

In a Dutch oven, brown bacon, onions, celery, and green pepper in oil. Add meat, salts, and pepper. Continue cooking until meat is browned on all sides. Add 1 quart water and simmer 1 hour. Add vegetables and simmer until meat and vegetables are tender (30 to 45 minutes). Add mushroom soup and the rest of the water. Mix flour with the 4 tablespoons water and add gradually to the stew, stirring constantly as stew thickens. Simmer 5 minutes. Serves 8.

Dutch Oven Stew

---

2 pounds venison, cubed
3 tablespoons bacon drippings
1½ quarts water
6 diced carrots
1 bay leaf
1 teaspoon salt
¼ teaspoon pepper
6 diced potatoes
6 ounces tomato sauce
3 medium onions, chopped
1 cup shredded cabbage
¼ cup water
2 tablespoons flour

Brown meat in a Dutch oven in bacon drippings. Add 1 quart water, carrots, bay leaf, salt, and pepper. Cover and simmer about 1½ hours. Add potatoes, tomato sauce, onions, and the rest of the water. (You may need more water to cover meat and vegetables depending on the size of your Dutch oven.) Simmer another 30 minutes and add cabbage. Cook about 20 minutes longer. Blend water and flour together to make a paste. Gradually add it to bubbling stew, stirring constantly until thickened. Recover and simmer until all meat and vegetables are tender. Serves 6 to 8.

Western Chili

2 pounds ground venison
¼ cup cooking oil
1 cup chopped onion
2 cloves garlic, minced
1 large green pepper, chopped
3 tablespoons chili powder
2 cups whole tomatoes
1 cup tomato sauce
1 cup water
½ teaspoon salt
1 tablespoon flour mixed with 2 tablespoons water
3 cups cooked kidney beans

Brown ground venison in oil in a Dutch oven until meat loses its pink color. Add onion, garlic, and green pepper. Cook for 5 minutes longer. Add chili powder, tomatoes, tomato sauce, water, and salt. Simmer for 2 hours. Add the flour paste and cook until mixture thickens. Add the kidney beans and cook another 15 minutes. Serve hot with French bread or hot biscuits. Serves 6 to 8.

Fruity Stew

2 pounds venison steak, cubed
2 tablespoons cooking oil
3 medium sweet potatoes, peeled and
 cubed
16 ounces canned whole tomatoes
1 medium onion, chopped
1 chopped green pepper
1/8 teaspoon nutmeg
1/4 teaspoon cinnamon
1 clove garlic, minced
1 teaspoon salt
1/2 teaspoon pepper
2/3 cup water
10 ounces canned corn (1 1/4 cups)
1 small zucchini, sliced
16 ounces canned peach slices (2 cups)

In a Dutch oven, brown meat in oil. Add sweet potatoes, tomatoes, onion, green pepper, nutmeg, cinnamon, garlic, salt, and pepper. Add water and mix well. Bake uncovered for 1½ hours at 350F°. Add corn and zucchini and bake 45 minutes longer. Drain peaches and add to stew. Stir well and heat through. Let stand for 5 minutes before serving. Serves 6 to 8.

Venison Chowder

1½ pounds ground venison
¼ cup chopped onion
2 tablespoons chopped green peppers
¼ cup chopped celery
3 medium potatoes, peeled and cubed (3 cups)
1½ tablespoons instant beef bouillon granules
½ teaspoon salt
2 cups water
3 cups milk
4 tablespoons flour
1⅓ cup grated cheddar cheese

Brown venison in a large saucepan with onion, green pepper, and celery. Add potatoes, beef bouillon granules, salt, and water. Cook until vegetables are tender (½ hour). Blend ½ cup milk with flour. Add to saucepan contents, stirring constantly. Add the rest of milk, stirring constantly. Cook until thickened. Add cheese and stir just until cheese melts. Serve immediately. Serves 6 to 8.

Tapioca Stew

2 pounds venison, cubed
1 tablespoon sugar
2 tablespoons quick tapioca
10¾ ounces condensed tomato soup
½ teaspoon salt
⅛ teaspoon pepper
¼ cup finely chopped celery
¾ cup water
1 diced potato
½ cup chopped red cabbage
½ cup chopped parsnips
½ cup chopped onion

Mix all ingredients in a Dutch oven. Cover and bake in oven at 250F° for 4 to 5 hours or until meat is tender. Add more water if needed. Serves 6.

Deerburger Soup

1½ to 2 pounds ground venison
1 cup diced onion
1 to 2 tablespoons cooking oil
1 cup diced potatoes
1 cup sliced carrots
1 cup condensed beef broth
¼ cup rice
1 bay leaf
½ teaspoon thyme
1 teaspoon salt
⅛ teaspoon pepper
1½ to 2 quarts water
29 ounces canned whole tomatoes (3½ cups)

In a large pot, brown meat and onion in oil. Add potatoes, carrots, and beef broth. Bring to a boil and add rice. Add the rest of the ingredients. Cover and simmer for 1½ to 2 hours. Just before serving, skim fat off the top. Serves 8.

Macaroni Soup

2½ pounds venison ribs
16 cups water
2 teaspoons salt
1 cup grated onion
1 cup grated carrots
½ cup grated potatoes
½ cup grated cabbage
¼ cup diced celery
1 teaspoon chopped parsley
½ teaspoon marjoram
½ teaspoon pepper
10¾ ounces condensed tomato soup
2 cups water
½ cup small shell macaroni

Place ribs in a large soup kettle with the 16 cups of water and the salt. Boil at medium heat for an hour and then simmer for about 8 hours. Strain liquid and return to kettle. Add onion, carrots, potatoes, cabbage, celery, parsley, marjoram, pepper, tomato soup, and 2 cups water. Remove ribs from liquid and cut as much meat as possible from the bones. Cut into small chunks and return to liquid. Boil the contents of kettle for 30 minutes or until vegetables are tender. Add macaroni and simmer until macaroni is cooked. Serves 6 to 8.

Barley Soup

1½ pounds venison bones
1 pound cubed venison
2½ quarts water
2 beef bouillon cubes
2 chicken bouillon cubes
1½ teaspoon salt
½ teaspoon celery salt or 1 stalk
   celery, finely diced
½ teaspoon pepper
⅛ teaspoon thyme
1 chopped onion
4 medium potatoes, cubed
3 sliced carrots
½ cup barley

Place venison bones, venison, water, bouillon cubes, salts, pepper, thyme, and onion in a large pot. Boil for about one hour. Remove bones and skim stock. Boil for about 1½ hours longer. Add potatoes and carrots. Boil another hour, adding more water to keep liquid to about 2 quarts. Add barley. Simmer about 40 minutes, stirring occasionally. Serves 6 to 8.

Meatball Sopa

1 medium onion, chopped
1 clove garlic, minced
2 tablespoons cooking oil
4 cups water
21½ ounces condensed beef broth
6 ounces tomato paste
2 medium potatoes, peeled and cubed (2 cups)
2½ medium carrots, sliced
1 beaten egg
3 tablespoons fresh parsley, chopped
¾ teaspoon salt
½ teaspoon leaf oregano
⅛ teaspoon pepper
1 pound venison
¼ cup rice

Cook onion and garlic in oil until onion is tender but not brown. Stir in water, broth, and tomato paste. Bring to a boil. Add potatoes and carrots and simmer for 5 minutes. In a mixing bowl, combine egg, parsley, salt, oregano, and pepper. Add ground venison and rice and mix well. Form mixture into small balls. Add a few meatballs at a time to boiling soup. Reduce heat and simmer about 45 minutes or until meatballs and vegetables are done. Serves 6.

Hobo Stew

2 large potatoes, sliced
1 cup chopped onion
½ cup chopped celery
½ teaspoon salt
¼ teaspoon pepper
15 ounces canned pork and beans (2 cups)
1 pound ground venison
10¾ ounces condensed tomato soup

Place potatoes, onion, and celery in the bottom of a greased casserole dish. Sprinkle with half the salt and pepper. Spread pork and beans over vegetables and place ground venison over beans. Sprinkle meat with remaining salt and pepper. Top with tomato soup. Cover and bake 2 to 2½ hours at 350F° or until meat and vegetables are thoroughly cooked. Serves 4.

GROUND VENISON

Venisonburgers

2 pounds ground venison
1 teaspoon onion salt
½ cup dry bread crumbs
⅛ teaspoon nutmeg
¼ teaspoon pepper
¼ teaspoon salt
¼ teaspoon marjoram
¼ teaspoon garlic powder, or 1 clove
  garlic, minced
1 egg
2 to 4 tablespoons melted butter

In a medium-sized bowl mix all ingredients except for the butter. Form mixture into 8 patties. Brush with melted butter and broil in oven or over outdoor coals. Turn once. Brush with butter again.

Foiled Venisonburgers

1 pound ground venison
Salt
Pepper
Garlic salt
4 tablespoons melted butter or margarine
3 medium potatoes, sliced
2 small onions, sliced
4 large carrots, sliced

Form 4 patties out of ground meat. Sprinkle with salt, pepper, and garlic salt. Tear off 4 pieces of aluminum foil large enough to wrap each patty generously. Brush the foil with melted butter or margarine. Put burgers on foil. Layer potatoes, onions, and carrots on top of each patty. Salt and pepper vegetables. Drizzle remaining butter or margarine over everything. Seal each packet of meat and vegetables. Grill over open coals about 20 minutes on each side or until everything is well done.

Marinated Patties

---

2 cloves garlic, minced
¼ cup cooking oil
¼ cup soy sauce
2 tablespoons ketchup
1 tablespoon cider vinegar
½ teaspoon pepper
1½ pounds ground
   venison
1 teaspoon salt
6 slices bacon

In a bowl mix garlic, cooking oil, soy sauce, ketchup, vinegar, and pepper togther. In another bowl mix meat, salt, and half the pepper together. Shape into 6 patties and place in glass dish. Pour garlic mixture over meat. Cover and refrigerate for 30 to 60 minutes, turning occasionally. Remove patties from marinade. Wrap a strip of bacon around outside edges of each patty and secure with toothpicks. Cook over coals or broil until done.

Wineburgers

1½ pounds ground venison
4 tablespoons red wine
3 tablespoons bread crumbs
6 strips bacon
2 to 3 tablespoons melted butter
Salt
Pepper

Mix meat with wine and refrigerate 1 to 2 hours. Shape into 6 patties. Wrap a strip of bacon around each, securing it with a toothpick. Brush patties with melted butter. Sprinkle with salt and pepper. Grill over coals or broil, basting with butter.

Roman Deerburgers

1½ pounds ground venison
¼ cup chopped parsley
1 clove garlic, minced
1 teaspoon leaf oregano, crumbled
¾ teaspoon salt
⅛ teaspoon pepper
2 tablespoons grated onion
2 tablespoons grated Parmesan cheese
4 thin slices mozzarella cheese
4 wedges Italian bread, toasted and buttered

Mix meat with parsley, garlic, oregano, salt, pepper, onion and Parmesan cheese. Shape into 4 patties. Grill over coals. Top each burger with mozzarella cheese when meat is cooked through. Remove when cheese is just melted and place on buttered toasted Italian bread. Serves 4.

Creole Burgers

1½ pounds ground venison
1 cup cooked rice
3 drops red hot sauce
3 tablespoons ketchup
¾ teaspoon salt
Pepper
4 hamburger buns
1 small green pepper, sliced into rings

Mix venison, rice, hot sauce, ketchup, salt, and pepper in a bowl. Make 4 patties. Grill over coals until done. Place on hamburger buns and top with green pepper rings. Serves 4.

Pocketburgers

1½ pounds ground venison
½ teaspoon onion salt, or ¼ grated
    medium onion plus ¼ teaspoon salt
½ teaspoon garlic salt, or 2 minced garlic
    cloves plus ¼ teaspoon salt
½ teaspoon parsley flakes
¾ cup cheddar cheese
4 thin slices of a large onion
Salt

Mix venison, onion salt, garlic salt, and prasley flakes together. Form into 8 thin patties. On half the patties place some grated cheese and an onion slice. Place a second patty on the top and press edges to seal. Grill outdoors over coals. Sprinkle with salt as they cook. Cook until well done. Serves 4.

Venisonburger Stack Ups

2 beaten eggs
¼ cup milk
1 teaspoon salt
1 teaspoon Worcestershire sauce
⅛ teaspoon pepper
1½ pounds ground venison
2 cups mashed potatoes
½ cup sour cream
¼ cup chopped scallions
2 tablespoons chopped pimiento
¼ teaspoon salt
3 slices American cheese

In a mixing bowl, combine eggs, milk, one teaspoon salt, Worcestershire sauce, and pepper. Add meat and mix well. Form into 12 patties. Place one patty in each of 6 individual greased casserole dishes. In another bowl mix potatoes in sour cream, onion, pimiento, and ¼ teaspoon salt. Spoon over patties. Top each casserole with one of the remaining patties. Bake uncovered at 375°F for 45 minutes. Cut cheese slices in half and place one half on each casserole. Bake two minutes longer or until cheese is melted. Serves 6.

Stuffed Super Deerburger

1¼ cup herb-flavored stuffing mix,
  crushed to ¾ cup
1 beaten egg
4 ounces (½ cup) canned mushrooms,
  drained
⅓ cup beef bouillon
¼ cup chopped green onion
¼ cup chopped toasted almonds
¼ cup chopped parsley
2 tablespoons margarine
1 teaspoon lemon juice
¾ teaspoon salt
2 pounds ground venison

Combine stuffing mix, egg, mushrooms, bouillon, onion, almonds, parsley, margarine, and lemon juice in a bowl until well mixed. Mix salt with venison. Divide meat in half. Pat half of the meat into a circle on a piece of greased 12×24 inch aluminum foil. Spoon stuffing mix onto circle. Cover with remaining meat, pinching edges to seal. Wrap entire meat patty in foil. Bake at 350°F for 45 minutes or until meat loses pink color. Serves 6.

Super Burger Supper

1 beaten egg
¼ cup quick-cooking rolled oats
1 tablespoon Worcestershire sauce
2 teaspoon minced dried onion
¼ teaspoon dry mustard
¼ teaspoon instant beef bouillon granules
1 pound ground venison
2 tablespoons cooking oil
10¼ ounces canned beef gravy
1¼ cups water
Cooked buttered noodles

In a large bowl, mix egg, oats, Worcestershire sauce, onion, mustard, and bouillon with venison. Shape into 4 patties. Brown patties in large skillet in oil until meat loses pink color. Pour canned gravy and water on burgers. Cover and simmer 15 minutes. Serve with hot buttered noodles.

Tuna and Venison Patties

2 pounds ground venison
1 cup grated carrot
1 cup sour cream
¼ cup chopped onion
6½ ounce can tuna fish, drained
⅓ cup dry bread crumbs
1 teaspoon salt
¼ teaspoon basil leaf, crumbled
¼ teaspoon thyme
⅛ teaspoon pepper
3 tablespoons cooking oil
1 cup dry white wine
2 tablespoons flour
½ cup chicken broth

Combine ground venison, carrot, one-half of the sour cream, onion, tuna, bread crumbs, salt, basil, thyme, and pepper in a large bowl. Mix well and shape into 6 to 8 patties. Brown patties in oil in a large skillet. In a blender combine wine, flour, and chicken broth. Blend until smooth. Pour wine mixture over patties. Cover skillet and bring to a boil. Reduce heat and simmer 30 minutes, basting patties with sauce several times. Remove patties to a heated platter. Add remaining ½ cup sour cream to sauce in skillet and heat slowly until hot, but not boiling. Spoon over patties and serve.

Everyday Meatloaf

2 pounds ground venison
¼ cup finely chopped onion
1 teaspoon salt
¼ teaspoon pepper
1 egg
1 cup uncooked oatmeal
½ cup tomato sauce
2 tablespoons Barbecue Sauce
    (recipe given on page 19)

Combine all ingredients. Mix well. Pack firmly in a greased
8½ × 4½ inch loaf pan. Bake in a 350°F oven for about 1½ hours
or until meat has lost all pink color. Serves 6.

Two-Day Meatloaf: Day 1

2 pounds ground venison
1 pound ground fresh pork
24 saltine crackers, crumbled
1 cup Chili Sauce (recipe given on
   page 19)
2 eggs
1 large onion, grated
1½ teaspoons salt
¼ teaspoon pepper
2 tablespoons chopped green pepper
¼ teaspoon celery seed
¼ teaspoon garlic powder
4 teaspoons Worcestershire sauce
¼ teaspoon dried savory
¼ teaspoon curry powder

Preheat oven to 350°F. Combine all ingredients in a large mixing bowl. Mix well and turn into 2 greased loaf pans. Bake for 1 to 1½ hours or until meat loses all pink color and is well browned. Serves 5 with leftovers.

Two-Day Meatloaf: Day 2

If you have a large family you may want to double the recipe given for day 1 so that you will have enough leftover meatloaf for day 2.

> Leftover meatloaf
> 1 loaf Italian bread
> 1½ teaspoons dried oregano
> ½ cup butter
> 1 to 2 tablespoons Parmesan cheese

Preheat oven to 350°F. Cut meatloaf into slices approximately the same shape as bread slices. Cut bread into ½ inch slices, keeping them in order. In a small saucepan melt the butter with the oregano and cheese. Brush butter mixture on both sides of meat and bread. Make a new loaf on a large sheet of aluminum foil by adding a slice of meatloaf between each slice of bread. Wrap securely in aluminum foil and heat in the oven for 20 to 30 minutes or until heated through. Serves 4.

Fiesta Pie

1½ pounds ground venison
1 tablespoon cooking oil
¼ teaspoon garlic salt, or 1 minced garlic clove
    plus ¼ teaspoon salt
¼ teaspoon dried minced onion, or 2 teaspoons
    minced onion plus ¼ teaspoon salt
¼ teaspoon celery salt, or 1 finely chopped
    celery stalk
2 teaspoons Taco Sauce (Recipe given on page
    20)
4 tablespoons ketchup
½ cup water
½ cup grated cheddar cheese
2 cups mashed potatoes
1½ teaspoons Parmesan cheese

Brown ground venison in skillet with oil, garlic salt, minced onion, and celery salt (or celery). When meat is brown, add Taco Sauce, ketchup, and water. Simmer 10 minutes. Put meat mixture in shallow baking dish. Sprinkle cheddar cheese over meat. Spread mashed potatoes on top. Sprinkle with Parmesan cheese over all. Bake at 350°F for 20 to 25 minutes. Serves 4 to 5.

Venison Meatloaf Supreme

2 pounds ground venison
½ pound loose pork sausage
¼ teaspoon garlic salt
1 large onion, finely chopped
½ teaspoon celery salt
¼ teaspoon dried parsley flakes
½ teaspoon dried thyme
1 cup dried bread crumbs
8 ounces (1 cup) tomato sauce
1 egg
½ teaspoon salt
¼ teaspoon pepper
½ tablespoon picante sauce (optional)
2 teaspoons Barbecue Sauce (recipe on
    page 19)

Place all ingredients except picante sauce and Barbecue Sauce in a large bowl. Mix well. Turn into an 8×8×2 inch buttered baking dish. Mix picante sauce and Barbecue Sauce. Spread over meat. Bake at 350°F for 1 hour or until done but still moist. Serves 6.

Sweet and Sour Deerloaf

2 pounds ground venison
¼ pound breakfast sausage
1 medium onion, diced
1 egg
1 medium green pepper, diced
¼ teaspoon garlic salt, or ½ large garlic
    clove, minced
¾ teaspoon salt
¼ teaspoon pepper
¾ cup dry bread crumbs
½ cup brown sugar
¼ cup cider vinegar
16 ounces (2 cups) tomato sauce
1 teaspoon soy sauce
2 teaspoons mustard

In a large bowl mix meats, onion, egg, green pepper, garlic salt, salt, pepper, and bread crumbs together. In a small bowl mix brown sugar, vinegar, tomato sauce, soy sauce, and mustard. Mix meat mixture with 1¼ cup tomato mixture. Form into a loaf and place in shallow baking dish. Pour remaining sauce mixture over loaf and bake at 350°F for about one hour. Serves 4 to 6.

Taco Chip Loaf

1½ pounds ground venison
1½ cups crushed taco-flavored
   chips
½ cup grated cheddar cheese
½ cup finely chopped onion
¼ cup finely chopped green pepper
¼ cup finely chopped celery
1 egg
1 cup evaporated milk
1 teaspoon salt

In a large bowl, mix all ingredients together thoroughly. Turn into a greased 2-quart covered casserole, spreading evenly around dish. Cover. Bake at 350°F for 1 hour. Serves 4 to 5.

Venison Meatballs

---

4 tablespoons butter
3 tablespoons chopped onion
1½ cups soft bread crumbs soaked in ¾ cup
    milk
1 pound ground venison
¼ teaspoon nutmeg
⅛ teaspoon pepper
½ teaspoon parsley flakes, or 1 teaspoon finely
    chopped fresh parsley
¾ teaspoon salt
1 egg
1 cup beef broth
1 tablespoon flour
2 tablespoons water

Melt half the butter in heavy skillet. Sauté onion. Place onions and butter in mixing bowl along with milk-soaked bread crumbs. Add venison, nutmeg, pepper, parsley, salt, and egg. Mix well and form into 1-inch balls. Melt remaining butter and lightly brown meatballs, adding more butter if needed. Add bouillion. Cover and simmer for 20 to 30 minutes. Remove meatballs. Mix flour and water and add to sauce remaining in skillet to thicken. Return meatballs to liquid and heat through. Serve hot. Serves 6.

Spanish Meatballs

2 pounds ground venison
2 large apples, peeled and
    shredded
2 lightly beaten eggs
2 medium onions, chopped (1½
    cups)
1½ teaspoons salt
½ teaspoon pepper
4 tablespoons cooking oil
1½ cups dry red wine
1¾ cups water
6 ounces (¾ cup) tomato paste
1 teaspoon crumbled basil leaf
½ teaspoon crumbled rosemary
    leaf
Cooked buttered noodles

Combine venison, apples, eggs, one cup of onion, salt, and pepper in a large bowl. Mix lightly. Shape into 1-inch balls. Heat oil in large skillet and brown meatballs on all sides. Remove balls from skillet when they are completely browned. Add remaining onion to skillet, sauté, stirring often until golden. Stir in wine, water, tomato paste, basil, and rosemary. Add meatballs. Bring to a boil and simmer 10 minutes. Serve with hot buttered noodles or rice. Serves 4 to 6.

Porcupine Balls

1 pound ground venison
½ cup onion, finely chopped
½ teaspoon salt
1 teaspoon pepper
½ cup uncooked instant rice
10¾ ounces condensed tomato soup diluted
    by 10¾ ounces water, or our recipe for
    Tomato Soup (on page 18)

Mix all ingredients in a bowl with half the soup. Shape into 1-inch balls. Place in large casserole. Pour remaining soup over meatballs. Cover and bake at 350°F for one hour. Serves 4 to 5.

Venison Meat Roll

1¼ cups biscuit mix
½ cup milk
1 teaspoon dry mustard
1 teaspoon parsley flakes
¾ pound ground venison
⅓ cup diced celery
⅓ cup diced onion
1 tablespoon Worcestershire sauce
¼ cup ketchup
2 unbeaten eggs
¼ cup quick-cooking rolled oats
1 teaspoon salt

Preheat oven to 425°F. Mix biscuit mix with milk, mustard, and parsley flakes. Roll to a 10×12 inch rectangle. Mix ground venison, celery, onion, Worcestershire sauce, ketchup, eggs, oats, and salt together in a mixing bowl. Spread meat mixture on dough, spreading to within ½ inch of edges. Roll up like a jelly roll, starting from long side. Moisten edge with a little water and seal. Bake in greased 9×13×2 inch pan for 30 to 35 minutes. Serve with sauce (recipe given below). Serves 3 to 4.

Meat Roll Sauce

¾ cup condensed tomato soup
¾ cup condensed cream of mushroom soup
¾ cup water
¼ teaspoon garlic salt

Stir all ingredients together and heat to boiling point.

Venison Corn Bread

1 to 2 tablespoons cooking oil
1 pound ground venison
⅓ cup chopped onion
1 clove garlic, minced
¼ cup ketchup
¾ teaspoon salt
Corn bread batter (recipe follows)
½ cup grated American cheese
2 tablespoons cold water
2 teaspoons cornstarch
1 cup canned tomatoes, cut up
2 tablespoons canned green chilies, diced
2 tablespoons chopped green pepper
1 teaspoon Worcestershire sauce

Preheat oven to 350°F. In a skillet, add oil and cook venison, onion, and garlic until meat is brown. Stir in ketchup and salt and set aside. Prepare corn bread recipe given below. Pour half the corn bread batter in a greased 8 × 12 × 2 inch baking dish. Spoon venison mixture over batter in dish. Sprinkle with cheese. Spread remaining batter over cheese. Bake uncovered for 30 to 35 minutes until corn bread is done. Let stand 5 minutes before cutting into squares. In a small saucepan, blend cold water with cornstarch until smooth. Stir in undrained tomatoes, chilies, green pepper, and Worcestershire sauce. Cook and stir until thickened. Serve sauce over cornbread squares. Serves 6.

Corn Bread Mixture

1 cup sifted all-purpose flour
¼ cup sugar
4 teaspoons baking powder
¾ teaspoon salt
1 cup yellow corn meal
2 eggs
1 cup milk
¼ cup softened shortening

Sift flour with sugar, baking powder, and salt. Stir in corn meal. Add eggs, milk, and shortening. Beat with electric beater until just smooth.

Venison Pie

---

1 pound ground venison
¼ cup grated onion
¼ cup finely chopped green pepper
½ cup dry breadcrumbs
½ cup tomato sauce
1½ teaspoons salt
⅛ teaspoon pepper
⅛ teaspoon ground oregano
Filling Recipe (given below)

In a large bowl thoroughly combine all ingredients. Pat mixture into the bottom and sides of a greased 9-inch pie pan. Prepare Filling Recipe that follows.

Venison Pie Filling

½ cup uncooked rice
1 cup water
½ teaspoon salt
1 cup tomato sauce
1 cup sharp cheddar cheese, grated

Combine rice, water, salt, and ¼ cup of the cheese. Spoon mixture into meat "crust." Cover with foil and bake at 350°F for 30 minutes. Remove foil and sprinkle with remaining cheese. Bake uncovered 15 to 20 minutes longer. Cut into wedges. Serves 4 to 6.

Venison and Pork Pie

---

2 pounds ground venison
½ pound ground fresh pork
¼ pound pork sausage
2 large onions, finely chopped
3 eggs
2 teaspoons salt
1 teaspoon pepper
2 cups oatmeal
2 tablespoons condensed milk
4 Pie Pastry crusts

In a large mixing bowl, mix all ingredients thoroughly. Place in a large heavy skillet and cook until all pink has disappeared from the meat. Place meat mixture in unbaked pastry shell (recipe on page 67). Cover with top crust. Brush with condensed milk. Bake at 400°F for 20 minutes. Makes 2 pies that serve 12.

Venison and Pork Pie Pastry

4 cups sifted all-purpose flour
1½ teaspoons salt
½ cup cooking oil
4 to 5 tablespoons cold water

Sift together flour and salt. Pour cooking oil and cold water into measuring cup. Add all at once to flour mixture. Stir carefully and form into ball. Divide into four portions and roll out on floured board to fill pie pan. Add meat filling to bottom crusts. Moisten rim of pastry. Cut slits for steam in top crusts and place on pies. Trim around edges and crimp edges for decoration.

Venison Stuffed Peppers

1 pound ground venison
¼ pound ground pork
⅓ cup cooked rice
½ teaspoon garlic salt, or 2 minced garlic
    cloves plus ¼ teaspoon salt
¼ teaspoon onion salt, or ¼ grated medium
    onion plus ⅛ teaspoon salt
¼ teaspoon salt
⅛ teaspoon pepper
2 eggs
5 to 6 medium peppers
15 ounces (2 cups) tomato sauce

Mix venison, pork, rice, the salts, pepper, and eggs in bowl.
Cut off the tops of the peppers and save. Clean out seeds
carefully. Stuff meat mixture into peppers and replace tops.
Place in a Dutch oven and add tomato sauce. Cover and bring
to boil. Simmer on low for about 1 hour. Add water if liquid
gets low. Remove and serve hot. Serves 5 to 6.

Stuffed Acorn Squash

1 medium acorn squash
½ teaspoon salt
2 tablespoons cooking oil
½ pound ground venison
2 tablespoons chopped onion
1 stalk celery, finely chopped
½ green pepper, finely
   chopped
2 tablespoons flour
¼ teaspoon salt
½ teaspoon poultry seasoning
¾ cup milk
¾ cup cooked rice
¼ cup grated cheddar cheese

Cut squash in half lengthwise. Scoop out and discard seeds. Sprinkle each half with ¼ teaspoon of salt. Place squash halves cut side down on greased baked dish. Bake at 350°F for 40 to 50 minutes. Meanwhile, add oil to a skillet and brown ground venison with onion, celery, and green pepper, cooking until meat loses all pink color. Stir in flour, salt, and poultry seasoning. Add milk. Cook and stir until mixture comes to a boil. Stir in rice. Remove from heat. Place cooked squash, cut side up, in greased baking dish. Fill with meat mixture. Bake 30 minutes more at 350°F or until squash is cooked through. Remove from oven. Top with cheese and bake 2 to 5 minutes or until cheese is melted. Serves 4 to 5.

Cabbage Rolls

---

12 large outside cabbage
   leaves
1 pound ground venison
¼ cup grated onion
2 tablespoons chopped parsley
¾ teaspoon salt
½ teaspoon thyme
¼ teaspoon garlic salt
⅛ teaspoon cayenne pepper
1 cup cooked rice
Butter or margarine
1½ cups tomato sauce

Cook cabbage leaves 3 to 5 minutes in boiling water. Drain and set aside. Mix meat, onions, parsley, salt, thyme, garlic salt, and pepper well. Mix in cooked rice. Place a portion of meat-rice mixture on cabbage leaf. Fold in ends and roll up, securing with a toothpick. Placed in greased baking dish. Dot each with butter or margarine. Pour tomato sauce over rolls and bake at 350°F for 1 hour. Serves 12.

Hash Brown Venison

2 pounds ground venison
2 tablespoons cooking oil
½ teaspoon onion salt, or 2 teaspoons
   grated onion plus ¼ teaspoon salt
¼ teaspoon salt
¼ teaspoon celery salt, or 1 finely
   chopped small stalk celery plus ¼
   teaspoon salt
⅛ teaspoon pepper
1 pound fresh or frozen loose hash brown
   potatoes
1 tablespoon powdered instant chicken
   bouillon
¾ cup water
2 tablespoons dry bread crumbs
4 tablespoons grated cheddar cheese

In a large skillet, brown venison in oil with the salts and pepper. Add hash brown potatoes and cook 5 minutes longer. Add bouillon and water and simmer 20 to 30 minutes. Turn into a serving bowl and sprinkle with bread crumbs and cheese just before serving. Serves 6 to 7.

Oriental Mix

1 pound ground venison
1 to 2 tablespoons cooking oil
1 cup cooked rice
½ cup diced celery
2 medium onions, chopped
¼ cup soy sauce
¼ teaspoon pepper
10¾-ounce can condensed cream
    of chicken soup
10¾-ounce can condensed cream
    of mushroom soup
2 cups water
1 cup bean sprouts
1½ cups Chinese noodles

In a large skillet, brown meat lightly in oil. Add rice, celery, onion, soy sauce, and pepper. Mix soups and water together in a large baking dish. Add meat mixture. Mix, cover, and bake 45 minutes at 350°F. Add bean sprouts on top and return dish to oven to bake for another 20 minutes. Sprinkle Chinese noodles over the top of casserole and bake for 15 minutes longer. Serves 4.

Noodle Medley

1 large onion, chopped
¼ teaspoon dried red pepper, crumbled
¼ cup diced green pepper
3 tablespoons cooking oil
2 cups canned whole tomatoes,
    undrained
2 pounds ground venison
Salt
1½ cups whole kernel corn
⅓ cup sliced pimiento-stuffed green
    olives
1 cup grated American cheese
8 ounces noodles

Sauté onion, red pepper, and green pepper in oil in a skillet until onions are translucent. Add tomatoes and cook 5 minutes. In another skillet, brown venison, adding salt to taste and a little more cooking oil if venison does not have enough fat in it to prevent sticking. When meat has lost all pink color, add the corn and half the sliced olives. Add the onion and tomato mixture and stir well. Add half the cheese and cook 5 to 10 minutes longer over low heat. Meanwhile, cook noodles according to package directions. Remove meat mixture from heat and stir in drained noodles. Pour mixture into a large casserole dish. Sprinkle top with the remaining cheese and olives. Bake uncovered for 45 minutes to an hour at 300°F. Serves 8.

Polka Dot Cups

1 beaten egg
¾ cup tomato sauce
¾ cup soft bread crumbs
½ teaspoon minced dry onion
¼ teaspoon garlic salt
¼ teaspoon fennel seed
½ teaspoon basil leaves
½ teaspoon oregano leaves
¾ teaspoon salt
⅛ teaspoon pepper
1 teaspoon instant beef bouillon granules
1 pound venison
1½ cups frozen, loose-pack hash brown potatoes,
    or 1½ cups finely diced fresh potatoes
2 to 4 tablespoons ketchup

Preheat oven to 375°F. In a large bowl, combine egg, ¼ cup tomato sauce, bread crumbs, onion, seasonings, and bouillon granules. Add ground venison. Mix well. Mix in potatoes. Divide into 8 portions and shape into balls. Place balls in greased muffin cups. Top with ketchup and bake 30 to 35 minutes. Serves 4.

Pot Luck Venison

1 medium onion, finely chopped
1 tablespoon cooking oil
1½ pounds ground venison
¾ teaspoon salt
1 cup sharp cheddar cheese, grated
10¾-ounce can condensed cream of
    chicken soup
5 ounces condensed cream of mushroom
    soup
2 cups cooked rice
4-ounce can button mushrooms, drained, or
    ½ pound fresh mushrooms sautéd in
    butter
1 small finely chopped green pepper
½ cup shredded cabbage
½ cup slivered toasted almonds
1 teaspoon butter
1 cup Chinese crisp noodles

In a skillet sauté onion in oil. Add meat and salt and cook until meat loses pink color. In a large casserole, mix meat with cheese, soups, rice, mushrooms, pepper, and cabbage. Place slivered almonds in a pie pan with butter or margarine in 350°F oven. When butter has melted, remove pan and stir, so that all the almonds are coated with butter. Return to oven and bake just until edges of nuts show a brownish color. Remove and mix into casserole. Top with Chinese noodles and bake 30 to 40 minutes at 350°F. Serves 6.

Fast Macaroni-and-Cheese Casserole

1½ to 2 pounds ground venison
1 tablespoon cooking oil
1 teaspoon dried minced onion
½ teaspoon garlic powder
¼ teaspoon salt
¼ cup tomato sauce
2 cups hot water
7¼-ounce package macaroni-and-cheese
  dinner

In a skillet brown meat in oil. Add dry seasonings, tomato sauce, water, packet of powdered cheese from macaroni-and-cheese dinner, and macaroni to skillet. Cover and simmer over low heat for 30 to 35 minutes, or until macaroni is cooked.

Jim's Casserole Delight

---

2 pounds ground venison
2 tablespoons cooking oil
¼ teaspoon garlic salt
½ teaspoon onion salt
10¾-ounce can condensed chicken noodle soup
10¾-ounce can condensed tomato soup
½ teaspoon chili powder
¼ cup bottled taco sauce (or the recipe for Taco
   Sauce given on page 20)
½ teaspoon parsley flakes, or 1 teaspoon finely
   cut fresh parsley
6 slices montery jack cheese, (1 × 3 × ¼ inch), or
   muenster cheese if desired

In a large, heavy skillet, brown venison in oil, seasoning with garlic salt and onion salt as it cooks. When meat has lost all pink color, add the remaining ingredients except for the cheese. Mix lightly and transfer into a large casserole. Place cheese on top of mixture and bake for 30 minutes at 350°F or until the meat mixture is hot and the cheese is melted. Serve on toast or rice. Serves 4 to 6.

Venison and Eggplant Casserole

1½ pounds ground venison
1 cup chopped onion
1 clove garlic, minced
3 tablespoons olive oil
1 cup Marinara Sauce (recipe given on page 21)
1 cup water
¾ cup dry red wine
1½ teaspoon basil leaf, crumbled
1 teaspoon oregano leaf, crumbled
1 medium eggplant, peeled and sliced (about 1 pound)
½ cup olive oil
½ cup grated Parmesan cheese
1 pound mozzarella cheese, thickly sliced

Brown venison with onion and garlic in 3 tablespoons olive oil in a large skillet. Add Marinara Sauce, water, wine, basil, and oregano. Cover and simmer 20 minutes. Sauté half the eggplant slices in ¼ cup of olive oil until limp and golden. Add remaining oil and sauté remaining eggplant. When all the eggplant is browned, place in a shallow baking dish. Spoon meat sauce over eggplant. Sprinkle Parmesan cheese evenly over casserole. Top with sliced mozzarella. Bake at 350°F for 20 to 30 minutes. Serves 6.

Porcupine Patties

2 pounds ground venison
2 large carrots, grated
2 large potatoes, grated
1 small onion, grated
2 eggs
4 tablespoons flour
½ teaspoon salt
¼ pepper
Cooking oil
10¾-ounce can condensed cream of
   chicken soup
1¼ cups milk

Mix venison, carrots, potatoes, onion, eggs, flour, salt, and pepper together in a large mixing bowl. Shape into 4 to 5 patties. Fry in a skillet with enough cooking oil to prevent sticking. When patties are well-browned and cooked through, place them in a greased casserole dish. Dilute chicken soup with milk and pour over meat. Bake in a covered casserole dish at 350°F for 35 to 40 minutes.

Busy-Day Venison Scallop

1 tablespoon cooking oil
½ pound ground venison
½ teaspoon salt
10-ounce package dried scalloped potatoes
4 ounces pimientos, drained and sliced
3 tablespoons chopped green pepper
10-ounce package frozen broccoli

Heat oil in a Dutch oven and brown venison, sprinkling salt on meat as it cooks. Make scalloped potatoes according to package directions. Add potatoes, pimientos, green pepper, and thawed broccoli to Dutch oven. Bring to a boil, cover, and simmer for 30 minutes or until potatoes are tender. Serves 4.

Taco Pizza

¾ cup warm water
1 package dry yeast
2½ cups flour
¾ teaspoon salt
2 teaspoons cooking oil
8 ounces tomato sauce
1 envelope taco seasoning
1 pound ground venison
½ cup canned diced green chilies
1½ cups grated cheddar cheese
1 cup shredded lettuce
1 medium tomato, chopped
½ cup crumbled corn chips

Dissolve yeast in warm water. Let it stand for 5 minutes. Add salt, flour, and oil. Mix into a soft dough. Spread dough evenly with fingers over a greased pizza pan. Mix tomato sauce and taco seasoning together, reserving ½ teaspoon of seasonings. Spread sauce on crust. Brown meat with remaining taco seasoning and add green chilies. Spread meat on pizza. Top with cheddar cheese. Bake for 20 to 25 minutes. Sprinkle with lettuce, tomato, and corn chips. Serves 4.

STEAKS
AND CHOPS

Venison Kabobs

1 to 2 pounds venison steaks (any cut), cubed
Bottled French dressing
Mushrooms
Pineapple chunks
Green peppers, sliced
Water chestnuts
Small onion chunks

Place cubed venison in a bowl. Pour enough French dressing over meat to coat well. Marinate for 1 hour or more. Skewer meat, mushrooms, pineapple, peppers, water chestnuts, and onions on skewers according to individual taste. Grill over charcoal, basting lightly with dressing.

Campfire Venison

---

3 tablespoons butter of margarine
1½ to 2 pounds venison steak
1 envelope onion soup mix (1⅜ ounce)
1 envelope tomato soup mix (1⅜ ounce)
½ teaspoon garlic salt
¼ teaspoon seasoned salt

Dot butter on pieces of aluminum foil large enough to wrap meat completely. Mix soup mixes and salts together in a small bowl. Sprinkle half of mixture on meat. Turn meat over and sprinkle remaining soup mixture on the other side. Dot with remaining butter and wrap securely in foil. Cook over open campfire or bake in 350°F oven for 1 hour. (Time would vary somewhat over campfire, depending on the temperature of fire and how close to the coals the meat is placed.) Serves 6.

Camper's Venison

2 pounds cubed venison
Salt
Pepper
Flour
4 to 6 tablespoons margarine
2 cups hot water
4 ounces canned mushrooms (½ cup),
    undrained
1 medium onion, sliced
8 ounces canned kidney beans (1 cup),
    undrained
3 medium carrots, sliced crosswise
6 ounces tomato sauce (¾ cup)
½ teaspoon leaf oregano

Salt and pepper meat and dredge in flour. Brown in margarine. Add water, vegetables, tomato sauce, and oregano. Cover and simmer slowly for two hours or until meat is tender. Serves 6.

Chicken-Fried Venison

2 pounds (4 pieces) venison steaks
1 beaten egg
¼ teaspoon garlic salt
¼ teaspoon onion salt
½ cup flour
Salt
Pepper
Cooking oil

Trim all fat from steaks and cut any visible membrane in meat to prevent curling during frying. Dip each piece in egg, then in a mixture of garlic salt, onion salt, and flour. Sprinkle with salt and pepper to taste and fry each slice in cooking oil until done. Serves 4.

Currant Venison

1½ pounds venison, cut into 1-inch cubes
Salt
Pepper
3 tablespoons butter or margarine
1 teaspoon chili powder
4 tablespoons sweet red wine
2 tablespoons red currant jelly
½ cup water

Sprinkle meat with salt and pepper. Brown meat in butter in a Dutch oven. Sprinkle chili powder on meat. Stir in wine, jelly, and water. Cover and simmer 1½ hours or until meat is tender, adding more water if necessary. Serves 4 to 5.

Chinese Pepper Steak

1 pound thinly cut venison steak
3 tablespoon olive oil
1 clove garlic, minced
⅓ teaspoon salt
½ teaspoon ginger
2 green peppers, sliced thin
2 tomatoes, peeled and sliced
1 cup bean sprouts
3 tablespoons cornstarch
¼ cup sherry, vermouth, or water
1 teaspoon sugar
Salt
Pepper
3 tablespoons soy sauce
3 scallions, thinly sliced

Slice steak across the grain as thinly as possible. In a skillet, brown strips in oil, garlic, salt, and ginger over moderate heat for 10 to 15 minutes. Add green peppers and tomatoes. Cover and cook over low heat for 5 minutes. Add the bean sprouts, cover, and simmer a few minutes longer. In a bowl mix cornstarch with either sherry, vermouth, or water and the sugar. Season mixture with salt, pepper, and soy sauce. Pour mixture over meat in skillet and bring to a boil slowly, stirring constantly. When cornstarch has thickened, add the scallions and cook 1 minute longer before serving. Serves 4.

Tarragon Venison

2 tablespoons margarine
2 tablespoons flour
1 cup light cream
¼ teaspoon salt
⅛ teaspoon pepper
2 tablespoons tarragon
½ teaspoon leaf basil
1 teaspoon brandy
8 slices cooked venison roast, each about
     6 × 4 × ½ inches

Melt margarine in a heavy skillet. Stir in flour gradually until mixture is golden brown. Reduce heat to low and stir in cream, mixing constantly until smooth. When mixture comes to a boil and thickens, add salt and pepper. Add tarragon, basil, and brandy. Lay venison slices in the sauce and heat through over low heat. Serve with rice. Serves 6 to 8.

Steaks à la Soupe

10¾ ounces condensed cream of
   mushroom soup
10¾ ounces condensed cream of
   chicken soup
½ cup dry red wine
¼ teaspoon onion salt
2 pounds venison steak (4 to 5 pieces)

Mix all ingredients except for the meat together in a casserole dish. Place steaks in mixture, turning to coat all portions of meat, making sure soup mixture covers meat. Add a little water if necessary. Cover and bake at 350°F for 1½ hours. Serves 4 to 5.

Barbecued Venison Chops

¼ teaspoon onion salt
½ teaspoon salt
¼ teaspoon pepper
3 tablespoons flour
4 venison chops or steaks (1½ to 2 pounds)
4 tablespoons oil
½ cup ketchup
¼ cup vinegar
½ teaspoon garlic salt
1 teaspoon liquid smoke
1 tablespoon Worcestershire sauce
Dash Tabasco sauce

SAUCE

In a small shallow bowl, mix together onion, salt, pepper, and flour. Dip chops or steaks in mixture and coat on all sides. Fry meat in oil until brown. Mix remaining ingredients in a small bowl. Pour over browned meat and simmer until meat is tender for 1 to 1½ hours. Serves 4.

*2-2-93 Boys did not like breading
Simply make Sauce & Bake
Simmering makes crusty bottom*

Chops in Gin

2 pounds venison steak
Salt
Pepper
2 tablespoons butter or margarine
3 tablespoons warmed gin
2 crushed juniper berries
⅛ teaspoon leaf basil
½ cup warmed heavy cream
Juice of ¼ lemon

First make Brown Sauce recipe given below. Sprinkle meat with salt and pepper. In a skillet, brown steaks in butter, cooking about 25 minutes on each side. Place steaks in shallow baking dish away from heat. Add gin to the skillet and ignite. When the flames die, stir and scrape the pan to get every-thing into the liquid. Add juniper berries, basil, and brown sauce, stirring over low heat. Slowly add cream and blend. When the mixture is heated through, add lemon juice and then pour liquid mixture over chops. If necessary, reheat the chops in a 350°F oven until warm, but don't let the sauce come to a boil.

Brown Sauce

2 tablespoons margarine
2 tablespoons flour
2¼ cups beef consomme or bouillion
Salt
Pepper

In a skillet melt butter and blend in flour, cooking and stirring over low heat until mixture is light brown. Gradually add consomme or bouillion, stirring until smooth. Bring to a boil and stir rapidly for 3 to 4 minutes. Lower heat and simmer for 20 minutes, stirring often to prevent sticking. Remove from heat and season with salt and pepper to taste. Serves 4.

Venison Bake

2 pounds venison steak
½ cup flour
1 tablespoon paprika
½ teaspoon salt
¼ teaspoon pepper
4 tablespoons oil
4 ounces canned mushrooms (½ cup)
1 beef bouillion cube
1 cup canned whole tomatoes
¼ cup chopped green pepper
2 stalks celery, finely diced
½ cup dry red wine
Parmesan cheese, grated

Pound meat with a meat mallet and cut into bite-sized pieces. Combine flour, paprika, salt, and pepper. Dredge meat in mixture and brown in hot oil. Remove to a baking dish. Drain liquid from mushrooms. Add enough water to mushroom liquid to make one cup. Heat mushroom liquid and water until it comes to a boil. Dissolve bouillion cube in mushroom liquid and pour over meat. Bake at 350°F for 45 minutes. Combine tomatoes, green pepper, mushrooms, celery, and wine. Remove meat from oven and pour tomato mixture into dish. Sprinkle with Parmesan cheese and bake 15 minutes longer. Serves 6 to 8.

Venison Beer Kabobs

1½ to 2 pounds venison steaks, cubed
12 ounces beer
¼ cup diced onion
2 tablespoons cooking oil
1 teaspoon salt
1 teaspoon curry powder
½ teaspoon ground ginger
⅛ teaspoon garlic powder
½ pound large fresh mushrooms
2 large green peppers, cut into chunks

Place meat in shallow dish. In a bowl, combine beer, onion, oil, salt, curry powder, ginger, and garlic powder. Pour over meat and marinate in a refrigerator for 4 to 5 hours. Drain meat, reserving the marinade. Skewer meat, alternating with mushrooms and peppers. Broil or grill over coals, brushing with marinade frequently. Serve immediately. Serves 4 to 6.

Rolled Venison

2 pounds venison round steak, (½ inch thick)
½ pound fresh mushrooms, sliced
1 small onion, chopped
3 tablespoons butter or margarine
1 cup dry breadcrumbs
1 tablespoon Worcestershire sauce
Salt
Pepper
Celery salt
Garlic salt
2 to 4 tablespoons cooking oil
1 cup dry red wine

Trim steak into a square shape. Sauté mushrooms and onions in butter. In a mixing bowl, mix mushroom and onion mixture with breadcrumbs and Worcestershire sauce. Sprinkle steak with salt, pepper, garlic salt, and celery salt. Spread mushroom mixture on meat and roll up loosely like a jelly roll. Tie in 3 or 4 places with string. Sear on all exposed sides in a Dutch oven. Pour in wine and bake covered in a 325°F oven for about 2 to 2½ hours or until tender. Serves 6.

Strip Steak

---

1 pound venison steak
½ teaspoon meat tenderizer
½ teaspoon leaf oregano
2 tablespoons cornstarch
½ teaspoon parsley flakes
3 tablespoons sherry
½ teaspoon salt
4 to 6 large onions, sliced
2 tablespoons cooking oil

Cut meat into strips ¼ inch wide and 3 to 5 inches long. Place strips in a bowl. Add meat tenderizer, oregano, cornstarch, parsley, and sherry. Sprinkle with salt. Mix and let stand at least 15 minutes. Separate onion slices into rings and fry in oil in a heavy skillet for 2 to 4 minutes, stirring constantly. They should still be somewhat crisp. Remove to a heated platter. Place steak strips into a skillet, stirring constantly for 2 to 4 minutes longer. Add more oil if needed. Put onions back into the skillet and heat through with meat. Serve at once. Serves 4.

Venison Cutlets

---

2 beaten eggs
1 teaspoon salt
⅛ teaspoon pepper
2 pounds venison round steak, ¼ inch thick
1½ cups Italian-flavored breadcrumbs
½ cup margarine

Beat eggs, salt, and pepper with a fork. Dip meat in egg mixture and then coat well with breadcrumbs. Let cutlets sit for 5 minutes. Then fry meat in margarine for 1 to 2 minutes on each side until golden brown and meat loses pink color. Serve immediately. Serves 6 to 8.

Deviled Venison Rolls

4 tablespoons hot water
2 tablespoons dry onion soup mix
3 tablespoons horseradish mustard
1½ pounds venison steak (cut very thin and
    scored with knife)
Salt
Pepper
4 ounces canned mushrooms, sliced
2 tablespoons butter or margarine

Preheat broiler. Cut steak into 4 portions. Mix water and dry soup and let stand 5 minutes. Stir in horseradish mustard. Sprinkle steaks with salt and pepper. Spread each steak with a fourth of the mustard mixture and top each with a fourth of the mushrooms. Roll up and fasten with toothpicks. Brush with melted butter. Broil until meat loses pink color throughout, turning and basting frequently with more butter. Serves 4.

Lima Bean Casserole

2 pounds venison, cubed
¼ teaspoon onion salt or 2 teaspoons
    minced onion
3 tablespoons cooking oil
¾ cup water
2 beef bouillon cubes
1 teaspoon salt
½ teaspoon ground cardamom
¼ teaspoon pepper
1 tablespoon lemon juice
8 ounces elbow macaroni
10 ounces lima beans, frozen
3 medium tomatoes, cut into wedges
1 teaspoon sugar
1 tablespoon parsley flakes or 3 tablespoons
    fresh parsley, finely chopped

Sprinkle meat with onion salt and brown in oil in large skillet. Stir in water, bouillon cubes, salt, cardamom, pepper and lemon juice. Cover; simmer 1 hour or until tender. Cook macaroni according to package directions and place in greased baking dish. Cook lima beans according to label directions and spoon over macaroni to make an edge around baking dish. Spoon meat in the middle and pour cooking liquid over everything. Top with tomato wedges overlapping each other. Sprinkle with sugar and parsley and bake at 350°F for 30 minutes. Serves 6.

Deer and Beer Bake

3 tablespoons flour
½ teaspoon salt
¼ teaspoon pepper
3 pounds venison, cubed
2 medium onion, diced
3-4 tablespoons cooking oil
4 cubes beef bouillon dissolved in 4 cups
   hot water
2 tablespoons tomato puree
2 cups beer
1 clove garlic, peeled
1 bay leaf
2 cloves
¼ teaspoon thyme
½ teaspoon salt
¼ teaspoon pepper
2 carrots, sliced crosswise
2 potatoes, cubed

Mix flour, salt, and pepper and dredge meat in mixture. Brown meat and onions in oil in Dutch oven, then add bouillon, tomato puree, and beer. Put garlic, bay leaf, cloves, and thyme in herb bag and add to pot. Cover and simmer 2 hours. Add salt and pepper, carrots, and potatoes and simmer covered about 45 minutes or until meat and vegetables are tender. Remove herb bag and serve. Serves 6 to 8.

Venison Stroganoff

1½ pounds venison round steak
¼ cup flour
½ large onion, minced
2 cloves garlic, minced
½ teaspoon salt
¼ teaspoon pepper
½ cup cooking oil
10¾ ounces canned beef broth
¼ cup dry red wine
1 cup sliced fresh mushrooms
1 cup sour cream

Slice steak into thin strips. Mix together flour, onion, garlic, salt, and pepper. Sprinkle flour mixture onto meat and brown in oil. When meat is browned stir in broth and wine, cover and simmer for 30 minutes. Add mushrooms and simmer 30 minutes longer or until meat is tender. Stir in sour cream and heat through. Serve over hot noodles. Serves 6.

Venison in a Wok

---

2 pounds venison round steak
1 cup cooking oil
⅓ cup soy sauce
¼ teaspoon ground ginger
⅛ teaspoon cayenne pepper
2 small onions, sliced
6 large mushrooms, sliced
2 stalks celery, chopped
1 green pepper, chopped
½ cup chicken broth
¼ teaspoon dry mustard
1 teaspoon cornstarch mixed with
    2 tablespoons water

Cut meat into strips about ¼ to ½ inch thick, against the grain. Marinate the meat in a bowl with ¾ cup oil, soy sauce, ginger, and cayenne pepper and refrigerate 3 hours. Cut vegetables immediately before cooking. Heat the remaining ¼ cup oil in wok (375°F if electric). Place meat in oil and stir-fry for 2 minutes. Push to the side and add the onions. Stir-fry 2 minutes longer and push to the side. Add mushrooms, stir-fry for 2 additional minutes. Add celery and fry for 2 minutes; then green pepper and fry for 1 minute. Add half of the marinade. Simmer 4 to 5 minutes. Dissolve cornstarch in water in a small dish. Add gradually to mixture in wok, stirring constantly until it thickens. Serve over rice. Serves 6 to 8.

Venison in Burgundy

4 tablespoons shortening
2 pounds venison, cut in 1-inch cubes
¾ teaspoon salt
1 clove garlic, minced
3 medium onions, sliced
½ teaspoon basil
Grated peel of half a lemon
1 teaspoon paprika
1½ tablespoons flour
1 cup dry red wine
1 cup canned beef broth
½ pound raw mushrooms, chopped
2 teaspoons parsley, finely chopped

Melt shortening in Dutch oven and brown meat lightly. Add salt, garlic, onions, basil, lemon peel, and paprika. Cover and simmer for 30 minutes. Sprinkle flour over meat and mix well. Add wine and beef broth and simmer for 1 hour. Add mushrooms and parsley, cover, and simmer 15 minutes or until venison is tender. Serves 5.

Grilled Pepper Steak

2 pounds venison round
    steak (cut 2 inches thick)
1 small onion, chopped
2 teaspoons thyme
1 teaspoon melted margarine
1 bay leaf
1 cup wine vinegar
½ cup cooking oil
3 teaspoons lemon juice
2 teaspoons unseasoned
    meat tenderizer
½ cup whole peppercorns,
    coarsely ground

Place meat in a plastic container. Combine the rest of the ingredients, except tenderizer and peppercorns, in a bowl. Mix well and pour over meat. Cover and marinate 8 hours or overnight. Drain off marinade and reserve. Pound pepper and tenderizer into meat. Grill over hot coals, basting periodically with marinade until meat is well done. Cut meat into ¼- to ½-inch strips and serve immediately. Serves 6 to 8.

Jelly 'n' Steak

---

2 tablespoons flour
½ teaspoon salt
¼ teaspoon pepper
2 pounds venison steak, thinly sliced
3 tablespoons cooking oil
1 cup heavy cream
Water

Jelly Sauce

---

2 tablespoons brandy
¼ teaspoon cinnamon
1 cup grape jelly

In a shallow bowl mix flour, salt, and pepper. Dredge meat in flour mixture and brown on both sides in oil in skillet. Add cream and enough water to almost cover steaks. Cover skillet and simmer for 1 hour. Meanwhile in the top part of a double boiler, heat brandy, cinnamon and jelly, stirring until smooth and heated through. Serve steak with jelly sauce. Serves 6 to 8.

Country Fried Venison

---

2 pounds venison steak
¼ cup flour
1 teaspoon salt
⅛ teaspoon pepper
3 tablespoons bacon drippings
¼ cup chopped celery
3 medium onions, sliced
1 tablespoon Worcestershire sauce
2 cups canned whole tomatoes

Cut venison into serving-sized pieces. Combine flour, salt, and pepper in a small bowl. Dredge each piece of meat in flour mixture. In large, heavy skillet, brown the meat on both sides in bacon drippings. Add celery, onions, and Worcestershire sauce; cook until vegetables are tender. Add undrained tomatoes and simmer, covered 1½ to 2 hours or until meat is tender. Serves 6.

Bold Charcoal Steak

---

12 ounces beer
½ cup chili sauce (recipe given on page 19)
¼ cup cooking oil
2 tablespoons soy sauce
1 tablespoon prepared mustard
½ teaspoon Tabasco sauce
¼ teaspoon liquid smoke
½ cup chopped onion
2 cloves garlic, minced
3 pounds venison steak
1 teaspoon salt
½ teaspoon pepper

In saucepan mix all ingredients together except steak, salt, pepper and simmer 30 minutes. Brush meat well with sauce. Cook over charcoal briquets, 20 to 30 minutes per side, or until well done, basting frequently with sauce. Season both sides of steaks with salt and pepper during the last few minutes of cooking and serve. Serve 6.

Steaks with Vermouth

Salt
Pepper
4 venison steaks, about 1½ inches thick
  (2-3 pounds)
Butter
4 tablespoons dry vermouth or dry white
  wine
4 tablespoons water

Salt and pepper steaks to taste. Brown steaks in butter in heavy skillet, approximately 5 minutes on each side. Add vermouth and cover. Simmer 20 to 25 minutes or until completely done. Add more water if necessary. Serves 4.

Cheese-Stuffed Venison

2 pounds venison round steak
¼ cup flour
¾ teaspoon salt
Pepper
1 cup chopped celery
½ cup chopped onion
1 teaspoon finely chopped fresh parsley
2 tablespoons butter
1 cup grated American cheese
½ cup soft bread crumbs
2 to 4 tablespoons cooking oil
1 cup water
1½ teaspoons instant beef bouillon
   granules
½ teaspoon dry mustard
½ teaspoon thyme
¼ cup cold water
2 tablespoons flour

Cut meat into serving-sized pieces. Mix ¼ cup flour, salt, and pepper. Pound flour mixture into both sides of each piece of meat. Cook celery, onion, and parsley in butter until tender but not brown and remove from heat. Stir in cheese and bread crumbs. Spread ¼ to ½ cup cheese mixture on each steak. Roll steaks up, jelly-roll style, and secure with toothpicks. Brown steaks in oil. Drain excess oil, then add 1 cup water, bouillon, mustard, and thyme. Cover and cook 2½ hours. Thoroughly blend ¼ cup cold water with 2 tablespoons flour and stir into pan drippings to make gravy. Serves 6.

Hunters Super Supper

1½ pounds venison, cut in 1-inch
   cubes
1 large onion, finely chopped
1 cup diced celery
2 to 4 tablespoons butter or margarine
½ cup rice
10¾ ounces canned condensed cream
   of chicken soup
10¾ ounces canned condensed cream
   of mushroom soup
4 ounces canned sliced mushrooms
4 teaspoons soy sauce
Salt
Pepper
1 cup peas
1 cup water
¼ cup dry red wine

Brown venison, onion, and celery in butter in a Dutch oven. In a large bowl mix together rice, canned soups, mushrooms, soy sauce, salt, and pepper. Add to Dutch oven and mix. Add peas, water, and wine. Simmer slowly for 1 to 1½ hours. Serves 6 to 8.

Vegetables 'n' Steak with Sour Cream

3 pounds round venison steak
3 tablespoons flour
¼ teaspoon garlic salt
¼ teaspoon celery salt
1 teaspoon salt
¼ teaspoon pepper
¼ cup shortening
⅓ cup red wine
1 medium onion, sliced
3 carrots, sliced
3 potatoes, sliced
1½ cups sour cream

Cut meat into serving-sized pieces. Mix flour with garlic salt, celery salt, salt, and pepper. Dredge meat in flour mixture and brown well on both sides in shortening. Add wine; cover and simmer 20 minutes. Place steaks in a shallow baking dish and reserve broth. Top each steak with a slice of onion, potato slices, and carrot slices. Pour sour cream and reserved wine broth over top. Cover tightly with foil and bake at 300°F for 2 to 2½ hours. Serves 6.

Butterfly Steaks

1 pound butterfly or backstrap steaks
½ cup flour
Salt
Pepper
Unseasoned meat tenderizer
Cooking oil

Flatten steaks and cut almost completely through horizontally to resemble a butterfly shape when opened. Pound lightly with a meat mallet on both sides. Sprinkle salt, pepper, and meat tenderizer on both sides of meat. Heat the oil in a large heavy skillet. Dredge meat in flour and fry in a half-inch of oil 2 to 3 minutes on each side. Serves 3.

Pressure-Cooked Stroganoff

1½ pounds venison, cubed
Flour, salt, pepper
2 tablespoons shortening
½ cup onion, chopped
½ teaspoon garlic salt
4 ounces canned mushrooms, reserving liquid
    (½ cup)
10½ ounces canned condensed tomato soup
1 tablespoon Worcestershire sauce
6 to 8 drops Tabasco sauce
½ teaspoon salt
⅛ teaspoon pepper
1 cup sour cream
1 teaspoon Parmesan cheese

Dredge meat in flour seasoned to taste with salt and pepper. Melt shortening in pressure cooker and brown meat well. Remove cooker from heat. Add onions, garlic salt, mushrooms and liquid, tomato soup, Worcestershire sauce, Tabasco sauce, salt and pepper. Mix well. Close cover securely. Cook at 15 pounds pressure for 15 to 20 minutes. Immediately cool cooker. Add sour cream and heat (do not boil) for 10 minutes in uncovered cooker. Sprinkle with Parmesan cheese and serve over wide noodles. Serves 6.

Stir-Fry Curry

1½ pound venison round steak, preferably
   from a very young animal
1 tablespoon soy sauce
1 medium onion
1½ cups beef broth
3 tablespoons flour
2 teaspoons curry powder
¾ teaspoon salt
3 tablespoons cooking oil
3 cups fresh broccoli buds, cut into 1-inch
   pieces
Chow mein noodles

Slice steak into thin strips across the grain. Place in bowl and sprinkle with soy sauce. Set aside. Cut onion into wedges and also set aside. Stir together broth, flour, curry powder and salt. Set aside. Heat wok or large skillet over high heat. Add 2 tablespoons of cooking oil. Stir-fry onion and broccoli 4 minutes. Remove vegetables. Add remaining oil to wok and stir-fry half of the meat for 3 minutes and push to side of wok. Repeat with remainder of meat. Stir flour-broth mixture and add to center of wok. Cook and stir until bubbly. Return vegetables to wok, stir, cover, and cook 3 minutes more. Serve over chow mein noodles.

Venison Goulash

3 pounds venison, cubed
½ cup floor
¼ cup margarine
1 cup chopped onion
1 tablespoon paprika
1 teaspoon salt
¼ teaspoon pepper
1 cup water
1 tablespoon tomato paste
1 green pepper, diced
1½ cups sour cream

Dredge meat in flour and set aside. Melt margarine in Dutch oven and sauté onions. Add meat and brown over medium heat. Season with paprika, salt, and pepper. Stir 3 tablespoons water, tomato paste, and green pepper into meat. Cover. Bring to a boil, then lower heat and simmer 2 to 2½ hours or until meat is tender, adding water as needed to prevent sticking. When meat is tender, add sour cream and heat through over low heat, stirring constantly. Serve over rice. Serves 6 to 8.

Steaks in Wine Sauce

2 to 3 pounds venison steaks
½ teaspoon garlic salt
¼ teaspoon salt
1 teaspoon dried minced onion
⅛ teaspoon pepper
10¾ ounces canned condensed cream of
  mushroom soup
¼ cup water
½ cup wine

Trim any fat from steaks. Place meat in a shallow casserole in a single layer. In a mixing bowl stir together salt, garlic salt, minced onion, pepper, mushroom soup, water, and wine. Pour over meat. Bake in 325°F oven for 2½ to 3 hours or until very well done. Serves 6.

Southern Style Venison

2 tablespoons butter
2 pounds venison, cubed
1 clove garlic, minced
½ teaspoon salt
⅛ teaspoon pepper
1 onion, grated
28 ounces canned whole tomatoes (3½ cups)
⅛ teaspoon baking soda
⅓ cup heavy cream
2 tablespoons flour
2 tablespoons red wine
2 teaspoons Worcestershire sauce
3 drops angostura bitters (optional)
1 teaspoon parsley flakes
2 tablespoons dry bread crumbs

Melt butter in a heavy skillet and brown meat, gradually adding garlic, salt, and pepper as meat cooks. When meat is brown, cover and cook 5 minutes longer, stirring several times. Add onion, cover and cook another 5 minutes. Add tomatoes and baking soda and simmer for 15 minutes. In a small bowl, mix cream and flour until smooth, and then add wine, Worcestershire sauce, and bitters. Pour cream mixture over meat and tomatoes. Stir until smooth. Cook 5 minutes more and turn into a buttered casserole. Top with parsley flakes and bread crumbs and bake 30 to 40 minutes in a 375°F oven. Serves 5 to 6.

Venison Ragout

3 pounds venison, cubed
3 tablespoons olive oil
3 large onions, chopped
3 to 4 garlic cloves, minced
½ pound bacon, diced
1 teaspoon curry powder
1½ quarts water
2 teaspoons bourbon whiskey
¼ cup beer
1 teaspoon salt
½ pound fresh mushrooms, sliced

Brown meat in olive oil in a Dutch oven. Add onions, garlic, and bacon. Cook until onions are soft and shiny, stirring frequently. Add remaining ingredients except for mushrooms; cover and simmer for 1½ hours or until meat is tender. Add mushrooms and simmer 20 minutes more. Serve over rice. Serves 8 to 10.

Venison and Vegetable Medley

½ teaspoon salt
¼ teaspoon pepper
2 pounds venison, cubed
2 tablespoons flour
5 tablespoons margarine
1 cup hot water
4 ounces canned mushrooms
1 medium onion, sliced
8 ounces canned kidney beans, drained
3 medium carrots, diced
1½ cups whole tomatoes
½ teaspoon dried oregano

Season meat with salt and pepper and dredge in flour. Brown meat in margarine in a Dutch oven. Add water, mushrooms, onion, beans, carrots, tomatoes, and oregano. Cover and simmer slowly for 2 hours or until meat is tender. Serves 6.

Zippy Ziti Casserole

1 pound venison, cubed
1 tablespoon shortening
16 ounces canned whole tomatoes,
    cut up (2 cups)
2 carrots, sliced crosswise
½ cup celery, chopped
½ cup onion, chopped
1 teaspoon salt
1 clove garlic, minced
1 teaspoon paprika
½ teaspoon chili powder
⅛ teaspoon pepper
2 cups water
1½ cups uncooked ziti

Brown meat in shortening. Add undrained tomatoes, carrots, celery, onion, salt, garlic, paprika, chili powder, and pepper. Cover; simmer for 1 hour. Add water and uncooked ziti. Bring to a boil. Cover and bake in oven 1 hour at 350°F, stirring occasionally. Serves 4.

Venison Casserole

2 pounds venison round steak (1 inch thick)
Flour mixture (see below)
4 tablespoons butter or shortening
4 medium potatoes, diced
2 medium onions, sliced
2 carrots, sliced
1 green pepper, diced
3 cups beef broth
¼ cup Parmesan cheese

Flour Mixture

½ cup flour
2 teaspoons salt
½ teaspoon pepper
⅛ teaspoon ground oregano
½ teaspoon garlic powder

Cut meat into serving-sized pieces. Dredge meat pieces in half of flour mixture and brown in butter or shortening. Transfer browned pieces to a 3-quart casserole. Place a layer of vegetables on the meat and sprinkle with half of the remaining flour mixture. Add the rest of the vegetables and sprinkle the remaining flour mixture on top. Pour broth over casserole, sprinkle cheese on top, and cover. Bake at 350°F for 1 hour. Uncover and cook 45 minutes longer or until vegetables and meat are tender. Serves 8.

Italian Style Steaks

2 pounds venison steaks (½ inch thick)
⅓ cup Italian style salad dressing
½ cup yellow cornmeal
Salt
Pepper
Cooking oil

Trim all visible fat from meat. Pour salad dressing over steaks and turn with fork so that each piece is coated with dressing. Marinate, covered, for 1 hour. Remove from marinade with fork and dredge in cornmeal. Salt and pepper each steak. Heat oil in a large skillet and sear meat on both sides. Reduce heat and cook until meat is thoroughly done. Serves 6 to 8.

Venison Steak with Ham

2½ pounds venison steak (½ inch thick)
1 teaspoon salt
¼ teaspoon pepper
½ cup margarine or butter
2 small onions, finely chopped
8 medium mushrooms, thinly sliced
8 thin slices boiled ham
8 tablespoons sour cream
2 tablespoons finely chopped parsley

Preheat oven to 350°F. Cut steak into 8 serving-sized portions. Melt ¼ cup butter or margarine in skillet. Salt and pepper steaks and brown for 10 minutes on each side. Remove meat from skillet and set aside. Melt remaining butter or margarine in skillet and sauté onions and mushrooms until soft and translucent. Remove from heat and prepare 8 pieces of aluminum foil large enough to wrap steak portions generously. On each piece place a steak, topped with a slice of ham, a generous tablespoon of the mushroom-onion mixture, 1 tablespoon sour cream, and a pinch of parsley. Wrap packets securely, place on a cookie sheet, and bake 25 to 35 minutes or until meat loses all pink color. Serves 8.

Steak and Rice

Soak Romertoff 15 min.

1½ pounds venison round steak (¾ inch thick)
1 cup uncooked rice
2 cups water
1 envelope dry onion soup
10¾ ounces canned condensed cream of celery
   soup
1 teaspoon salt
⅛ teaspoon pepper

Cut steak into serving-sized pieces and place in a casserole.
Mix together remaining ingredients and pour over meat.
Cover and bake at 400°F for 1½ hours or until steak is tender.
Serves 6.

12/2/91 KK likes add a little more liquid

Uintah Swiss Steak

¼ cup flour
1½ pounds round steak (½ to ¾ inches
   thick)
½ teaspoon salt
¼ teaspoon pepper
½ teaspoon garlic salt
2 to 4 tablespoons cooking oil
3 large onions, sliced
1 stalk celery, chopped
1 cup canned whole tomatoes
2 tablespoons Worcestershire sauce
1 to 2 tablespoons flour mixed with 2 to 4
   tablespoons water

Dredge meat in flour seasoned with salt, pepper, and garlic salt. Heat oil in skillet and sear meat until well browned on both sides. Add the remaining ingredients, except flour paste. Bring to a boil, cover, and reduce heat. Simmer 1½ hours or until meat is tender. Remove steak from sauce to a platter and thicken sauce slightly with flour-water mixture. Serve sauce separately. Serves 6.

Venison Pastry

½ pound venison steak
1 veal or 2 lamb kidneys
1 large potato
1 tablespoon finely chopped onion
Salt
Pepper

Pastry

---

1 cup biscuit mix
⅓ cup milk
1 slightly beaten egg yolk

Preheat oven to 425°F. Cut the steak, kidney, and peeled potato into 1-inch cubes. Add chopped onion and season with salt and pepper. Thoroughly blend biscuit mix and milk and roll out to ¼ inch thickness. Cut into 6-inch rounds. Place a quarter of the meat mixture on each round and fold over. Crimp edges with tines of fork, and brush pastries with slighly beaten egg yolk. Bake 10 minutes at 425°F; reduce heat to 350°F and bake 50 minutes longer.

Cantonese Steak

---

1 pound venison steak
½ teaspoon instant meat tenderizer
2 tablespoons cornstarch
4 tablespoons sherry
½ teaspoon soy sauce
Salt
4 to 6 large onions, sliced
2 to 4 tablespoons cooking oil

Cut meat into strips ¼ inch wide and 2 to 4 inches long and place in a bowl. Add tenderizer, cornstarch, and sherry. Sprinkle with salt. Mix and let stand at least 15 minutes. Separate onion slices into rings and fry in hot oil in a heavy skillet or wok over medium heat for 2 to 4 minutes, stirring constantly. They should be still somewhat crisp. Remove to heated platter. Place steak strips in hot skillet, adding more oil if necessary, and stir constantly for 2 to 4 minutes. Put onions back into skillet and mix with meat. Serve at once, with rice. Serves 3 to 4.

Bayou Venison

2 pounds venison steaks
¾ teaspoon lemon-pepper seasoning
½ teaspoon salt
¼ teaspoon cayenne pepper
1 clove garlic, minced
3 slices lime, chopped
2 cups chopped onion
1 cup chopped green pepper
1 teaspoon soy sauce
1 cup sauterne
½ teaspoon parsley flakes

Season meat with lemon pepper, salt, cayenne pepper, and garlic. Place meat in Dutch oven and add rest of the ingredients. Cover, bring quickly to a boil, and then reduce heat and simmer until meat is tender, about 1½ to 2 hours. Serves 4 to 6.

Lemon Steaks

---

2 pounds venison steaks
Juice of 1 lemon, plus 2 to 3 tablespoons
lemon juice
½ teaspoon garlic salt
½ teaspoon onion salt
⅛ teaspoon pepper

Line a shallow baking dish with enough aluminum foil to cover meat while cooking. Place steaks in a single layer on foil. Squeeze the juice from a half lemon over exposed sides of meat and sprinkle with garlic salt, onion salt, and pepper. Turn steaks over and season with other half lemon, salts, and pepper. Seal aluminum foil around steaks and bake at 400°F for 50 minutes. Uncover steaks; pour 2 to 3 tablespoons lemon juice over meat and broil for 10 minutes. Serves 6 to 8.

ROASTS

Venison Roast Crowned with Stuffing

4 pounds venison roast
½ cup very soft butter or margarine
2 cups dry breadcrumbs
1 teaspoon salt
½ teaspoon pepper
½ medium onion, chopped
1 teaspoon sage
½ teaspoon dried leaf thyme
½ cup chopped celery
1 teaspoon parsley flakes
1 cup unpeeled and coarsely chopped
   tart apple
1 beef bouillon cube, dissolved in 1
   cup hot water
4 strips bacon

Place roast on a large sheet of heavy-duty aluminum foil. Spread butter or margarine over top and sides of meat. In mixing bowl combine breadcrumbs, salt, pepper, onion, sage, thyme, celery, parsley flakes, apples, and bouillon. Mix well. Pat stuffing on top of meat with fingers. Arrange bacon slices on top of stuffing. Fold foil around roast, leaving some air inside but sealing all seams with a double fold. Roast in a 350°F oven for 2½ to 3½ hours or until tender and well done. Slice meat and serve accompanied by stuffing. Serves 8 to 10.

Sweet and Sour Venison

3 pounds venison roast
6 tablespoons cooking oil
1 teaspoon salt
1¼ cups dark brown sugar
2 teaspoons prepared mustard
2 tablespoons vinegar
¼ cup water

In a Dutch oven sear meat on all sides in hot oil. Combine salt, brown sugar, mustard, and vinegar to make a thick paste and spread paste all over roast. Carefully pour water into bottom of pan. Cover roast and bake at 350°F for 2 to 3 hours, or until meat loses all pink color. Baste frequently with pan drippings, adding more water if needed. Serves 6.

Venison Pot Roast

1 medium onion, sliced
2 bay leaves
½ teaspoon leaf oregano
¼ teaspoon pepper
½ teaspoon salt
4 cups red wine
3½ to 4 pounds venison roast
2 to 4 tablespoons shortening

Mix together onion, bay leaf, oregano, pepper, salt, and red wine. Marinate meat in this mixture for 3 hours, turning frequently. Remove meat and pat dry. Brown meat in shortening in large Dutch oven. Roast in slow oven (300°F) for 4 hours or until well done, basting with marinade every 15 to 20 minutes. Serves 8.

Venison in Beer

4 to 5 pounds venison roast
¾ to 1 teaspoon salt
½ teaspoon pepper
6 slices bacon
2 beef bouillon cubes
¼ cup boiling water
1 onion, sliced
2 bay leaves
12 ounces beer
Flour

Salt and pepper roast and place in 9 × 11 pan lined with sufficient aluminum foil to cover roast. Lay bacon on top of meat. Dissolve bouillon cubes in boiling water. Add onion, bay leaves, bouillon, and beer. Seal with foil and roast 3 to 3½ hours in a 350°F oven or until completely done. If gravy is desired, thicken pan juices with flour. Serves 6.

Venison Sauerbraten

3½ pounds venison roast
1 teaspoon salt
½ teaspoon pepper
2 medium onions
1 medium carrot, sliced
1 large stalk celery, sliced
4 whole cloves
4 crushed peppercorns
2 bay leaves
2 cups vinegar
¼ cup butter or margarine (½ stick)
12 small gingersnaps, crushed
1 tablespoon sugar
2 tablespoons flour mixed with ¼
    cup water (optional)

Begin to prepare several days ahead. Season meat with salt and pepper and place in a glazed crock or in a stainless steel or glass bowl. Add onions, carrots, celery, cloves, peppercorn, bay leaves, and vinegar. Cover and refrigerate for 3 days, turning several times a day. When ready to cook, drain meat and wipe dry. Strain and reserve marinade. Melt butter in Dutch oven and sear meat on all sides. Add the marinade and bring to a boil. Lower heat and simmer covered 2 to 3 hours or until meat in cooked through and very tender. Remove meat to heated platter and cover with foil to keep warm. Bring pan juices to boil. Add gingersnaps and sugar. Stir over medium heat until thickened. If necessary, add flour and water mixture as needed, to thicken further and cook until gravy desired thickness is reached. Pour some of the sauce over the sauerbraten, reserving the rest to serve when roast is sliced. Serve with potato dumplings. Serves 6-8.

Potato Dumplings

---

6 medium potatoes, peeled
    and coarsely grated
4 slices white bread
½ teaspoon salt
1 cup cold water or milk
2 tablespoons parsley flakes
1 medium onion, peeled
    and coarsely grated
2 eggs, well beaten
¼ cup flour
2 quarts boiling salted water

Place grated potatoes in a fine sieve and press with paper towels to remove as much moisture as possible. Trim crusts from bread and soak in water or milk for 2 minutes; squeeze out water and mix bread with salt, parsley, onion, potato, and eggs. Shape into balls about 1½ inches in diameter. Roll in flour and drop dumplings into boiling water, cover, reduce heat, and boil gently for 12 to 15 minutes. Drain in sieve or colander. Serve with sauerbraten.

Curried Venison

1½ medium onions, grated
4 stalks celery, chopped
2 medium apples, grated
4 to 6 tablespoons cooking oil
3 pounds cooked venison, cubed
2 teaspoons salt
⅛ teaspoon pepper
2 teaspoons curry powder
2 cups beef broth
¼ teaspoon ginger
⅛ teaspoon Tabasco sauce
1 tablespoon Worcestershire sauce
2 tablespoons flour
¼ cup cold water
1 cup milk
1 egg yolk, well beaten

In heavy skillet sauté onions, celery, and apples in oil until lightly brown. Add meat, salt, pepper, curry powder, beef broth, ginger, Tabasco, and Worcestershire sauce. Mix well. Bring to a boil and simmer, covered, for 20 to 25 minutes. Mix flour to a smooth paste with the water and add a little at a time, stirring mixture constantly until thick. Simmer 5 minutes. Remove from heat and let stand for 1 hour so seasonings can permeate meat. Reheat and add milk and egg yolk gradually, stirring constantly. Heat just to boiling and serve over rice. Serves 8 to 10.

Leftover Venison Stroganoff

1 medium onion, chopped
2 tablespoons cooking oil
3 cups cooked venison roast, cubed
10¾ ounce can condensed tomato soup
4 ounce can chopped mushrooms
¾ teaspoon sugar
1 cup sour cream

Sauté onion in oil until tender in large skillet. Add venison cubes and brown lightly. Stir in tomato soup, mushrooms, mushroom liquid, and sugar. Cover; simmer 30 minutes. Stir in sour cream and heat just to boiling point (do not boil). Serve over hot buttered noodles or rice. Serves 4 to 6.

Bacon Roast

3½ to 4 pounds venison roast
½ teaspoon salt
¼ teaspoon pepper
¼ teaspoon onion salt
¼ teaspoon garlic salt
4 slices bacon

Rub seasonings into roast. Lay bacon strips over meat. Wrap meat securely in aluminum and bake at 325°F for 2½ to 3½ hours, or until meat is tender and loses pink color. Serves 6 to 8.

Lois's Pot Roast

1 small onion, sliced
2 cloves garlic, peeled and halved
   lengthwise
1 bay leaf
½ teaspoon dried rosemary
¼ teaspoon dried basil
¼ teaspoon pepper
4 cups white wine
4 to 5 pounds venison roast (any cut)
4 tablespoons cooking oil
¾ teaspoon salt

Mix first 7 ingredients together. Marinate meat in this mixture for 3 hours, turning frequently. Remove meat and dry. Brown meat in cooking oil in large Dutch oven. Sprinkle with salt. Roast, covered, in a 325°F slow oven for 4 hours, or until well done, basting with marinade every 15 or 20 minutes. Add enough additional marinade to the pan to keep meat from sticking to the pan while cooking. Serves 6 to 8.

"Milk" Venison

2 to 3 pounds venison roast
1 cup milk
3 tablespoons shortening
¼ teaspoon garlic salt
¼ teaspoon onion salt
¼ teaspoon salt
⅛ teaspoon pepper
10¾ ounces canned condensed
   cream of chicken soup
10¾ ounces water (soup can full)
¼ cup red wine

Place venison in milk to cover and let soak for at least 1 hour. This mellows stronger venison. Rinse milk from meat. Sprinkle with dry seasonings. Brown meat in shortening over high heat. Mix soup, water, and wine and pour over browned meat. Cover and bake at 350°F for 2 hours or until tender. Serves 4.

Venison One-Pot Meal

3 to 4 pounds venison roast
2 cups water
1 bay leaf
⅛ teaspoon thyme
⅛ teaspoon basil
¼ teaspoon pepper
¾ teaspoon salt
1 large stalk celery, diced
4 carrots, sliced
4 small turnips, quartered
6 small potatoes, quartered
1 small onion, sliced
4 slices bacon
½ cup sour cream

Place meat in Dutch oven. Add water, seasonings, and vegetables. Lay bacon on top of meat. Cover pan tightly and simmer until vegetables are cooked and meat is tender, 3 to 3½ hours. Remove meat to platter. Add sour cream to pan drippings and heat through but do not boil. Serve sauce immediately with meat. Serves 8.

Cider Venison

4 pounds venison roast
1 tablespoon cooking oil
1¼ teaspoon pepper
½ teaspoon salt
¼ cup flour
1 teaspoon ground oregano
½ teaspoon thyme
1 teaspoon rosemary
½ teaspoon garlic salt
1 cup apple cider or juice
1 cup water
Flour

Cut several slits in the roast and rub with oil. In a small bowl, mix pepper, salt, flour, oregano, thyme, rosemary, and garlic salt. Add just enough water to make a paste. Rub paste into meat, working into each slit. Place meat in baking dish containing apple cider and water. Bake uncovered in a 325°F oven for one hour. Baste with juices and cider mixture. Cover. Roast another 2½ hours or until well done, basting every 15 or 20 minutes. Slice thin and make gravy from pan juices by thickening with a little flour, if desired. Serves 6 to 8.

Barbecued Roast

3 to 4 pound venison roast
2 tablespoons shortening
½ bottle barbecue sauce (recipe on page 19,
    or use one of your favorite recipes)

Brown meat in shortening on all sides in a heavy Dutch oven. Pour barbecue sauce over the roast. Cover and bake for 3 to 3½ hours in a 350°F oven, basting with pan drippings from time to time. Serves 6 to 8.

Hungarian Venison Roast

5 pounds venison roast (any cut)
Several strips salt pork
2 cloves garlic, sliced
Salt and pepper
Flour
3 tablespoons olive oil
2 onions, coarsely chopped
2 carrots, sliced
1 potato, chopped
1 teaspoon marjoram
1 stalk celery, chopped
1 teaspoon minced parsley
½ cup beef bouillon
½ cup dry white wine
½12.09½ cup sour cream
1 tablespoon paprika

Cut several deep slits in roast. Using a knife, push the strips of salt pork into the slits. Cut garlic lengthwise into thin slivers and push also into the slits. Rub the roast with salt and pepper and roll in flour. Sear quickly on all sides in olive oil in a Dutch oven. Add onions, carrots, potato, marjoram, parsley, celery, bouillon, and wine to pot. Cover and simmer for 3 to 3½ hours or until done, adding more water if necessary. When meat is done remove to a hot platter and add sour cream to broth and heat through. Serve roast with sauce poured over each piece. Sprinkle with paprika for garnish just before serving. Serves 10.

Venison and Dumplings

¾ pound venison roast
2 tablespoons cooking oil
2 cups whole tomatoes
¼ cup dry red wine
½ teaspoon salt
½ teaspoon rosemary
¼ teaspoon pepper
¼ teaspoon garlic salt or 1 clove
    garlic, finely minced

Brown meat on all sides in oil. Add undrained tomatoes, wine, salt, rosemary, pepper, and garlic salt. Cover and simmer until meat is tender, 2 to 3 hours, adding more water if necessary. Make dumplings (see below) and drop by spoonfuls into cooking meat mixture. Return to boiling. Reduce heat and simmer 12 to 15 minutes. Remove meat and dumplings and serve pan drippings as a sauce with the meal.

Dumplings

1 cup flour
2 tablespoons fresh minced parsley
2 teaspoons baking powder
½ teaspoon salt
1 egg
¼ cup milk
2 tablespoons melted margarine

Mix together flour, parsley, baking powder, and salt. Combine egg, milk, and melted margarine. Add to flour mixture, stirring just until blended. Then drop by spoonfuls into cooking meat mixture and proceed as directed above.

Roast Supreme

½ cup vinegar
2 cups water
3 to 4 pounds venison roast
½ cup dry wine
1 teaspoon meat tenderizer
¾ to 1 teaspoon salt, or to taste
1 teaspoon pepper
½ teaspoon garlic powder
6 thin round slices of fresh lemon
3 strips bacon, cut in half

Soak roast overnight in water and vinegar. Rinse with fresh water and pat dry. Brush on half the wine. Sprinkle tenderizer, salt, pepper, and garlic powder on meat. Place lemon slices on top of roast and top with bacon, secured by toothpicks. Roast in 275°F oven 4 to 5 hours. Baste often with sauce (see below) while baking. Serves 6 to 8.

Sauce for Roast Supreme

¼ cup butter
¼ cup honey
½ cup frozen orange juice concentrate
½ teaspoon rosemary

Mix all ingredients together in a small bowl.

Down Home Venison

6 thick slices of leftover cooked venison roast,
   cut 1 inch thick
2 tablespoons olive oil
¼ to ½ teaspoon garlic salt
18 ounces canned baked beans
1 cup mild barbecue sauce or use
   homemade barbecue sauce (recipe on
   page 19)
4 strips bacon, fried crisp and crumbled

Brush oil on both sides of venison. Sprinkle with garlic salt. Grill over coals 8 to 10 minutes or until well browned on each side. Meanwhile, heat beans until hot. Turn meat and spread beans carefully on one side of meat. Spoon barbecue sauce over beans. Cook until second side is well browned. Then carefully lift each piece onto warmed plates. Serves 6.

Savory Roast

---

4 to 5 pounds venison roast
1 cup light cream
1 teaspoon savory
½ teaspoon parsley flakes or
   1 teaspoon finely chopped
   fresh parsley
1 teaspoon salt
¼ teaspoon pepper
1 onion, sliced
1 cup sliced fresh mushrooms

Lay roast on large sheet of aluminum foil placed in a shallow baking dish. Pour cream over roast. Sprinkle with savory, parsley, salt, and pepper. Add onion and mushrooms. Wrap foil tightly to seal and roast in 350°F oven for 2½ to 3 hours or until well done. Serves 8 to 10.

Busy-Day Venison

3 pounds venison roast
½ medium onion, sliced
½ cup ketchup
⅓ cup lemon juice
¼ teaspoon salt
¼ teaspoon garlic salt
Pepper

Place roast in electric crock pot. Add all ingredients and simmer 6 to 8 hours or until tender. Serves 4 to 5.

Venison Platter

4 pound venison roast
¼ teaspoon garlic salt
3 tablespoons cooking oil
2 medium onions, sliced thin
15½ ounces canned prepared
    sandwich sauce
1½ cups water
8 ounces egg noodles
¼ cup chopped parsley

Trim any fat from meat. Sprinkle garlic salt on meat and sear meat in oil on all sides in Dutch oven. Stir in onion and saute slightly. Add sandwich sauce and boiling water. Simmer 3 to 3½ hours or until tender, turning meat occasionally. When roast is done, cook noodles according to package directions. Drain and sprinkle parsley over noodles. Place meat on platter and spoon noodles around meat. Pour part of sauce over meat and serve the rest with meat. Serves 6.

Deer Camp Venison

1 barked green willow branch
2 to 3 pounds venison roast
½ cup parsley
4 cloves garlic, minced
½ teaspoon leaf oregano
½ cup olive oil
½ teaspoon salt
⅛ teaspoon pepper

Thread venison onto willow branch or onto a backyard rotisserie. Combine remaining ingredients and baste roast with mixture. Turn and baste frequently as meat cooks. Cook about 1½ to 2½ hours, or until meat loses pink color. Cooking time will vary due to variation in heat of open fires and other factors. Serves 4 to 6.

Dutch Oven Roast Venison

3 pounds venison roast
⅓ cup cider vinegar
3 tablespoons flour
½ teaspoon salt
¼ teaspoon pepper
2 to 3 tablespoons bacon drippings
3 strips bacon, cut in half
1 onion, sliced and separated into rings
½ cup hot water
10¾ ounces canned condensed tomato
    soup
⅓ teaspoon garlic salt
¼ teaspoon leaf basil

Soak a clean cloth in vinegar and wipe the roast. In Dutch oven, sear meat on all sides in bacon drippings. Lay strips of bacon across roast, securing with toothpicks. Hang the rings of onion slices over the toothpicks. Add the hot water, tomato soup, garlic salt, and basil to Dutch oven. Cover and simmer for 2 to 3 hours, or until tender. Thicken pan juices to make gravy if desired. Serves 6 to 8.

Crabapple Venison

5 to 6 pounds leg of venison
½ to ¾ pounds salt pork, thinly sliced
Salt
Pepper
¼ cup orange juice
2 tablespoons lemon juice
¼ teaspoon powdered allspice
2 tablespoons melted margarine
2 tablespoons orange juice
¼ cup crabapple jelly

Season meat with salt and pepper and cover with salt pork. Mix orange juice, lemon juice, and allspice together. Sear meat in preheated 450°F oven for 15 minutes. Reduce heat to 350°F and cook covered for 4 hours or until meat is well done, basting frequently with juice mixture. Half an hour before meat is done, remove the salt pork. Combine margarine, orange juice, and jelly, brush meat with glaze, and continue roasting uncovered, basting with glaze several times. Serves 10.

ETHNIC
RECIPES

Venison Moussaka

16 ounces canned green beans (2 cups)
2 pounds ground venison
8 ounces tomato sauce (1 cup)
½ teaspoon garlic salt or 2 cloves garlic,
*   minced, plus ¼ teaspoon salt*
⅛ teaspoon cinnamon
6 ripe olives, sliced
2 tablespoons ripe olive juice
2 cups ricotta or cottage cheese
2 eggs
½ cup Parmesan cheese
½ teaspoon parsley flakes or 1 teaspoon
*   fresh parsley, finely chopped*

Put green beans in a buttered baking dish. Brown meat in heavy skillet. Add tomato sauce, garlic salt, and cinnamon. Spread meat mixture over the beans. Combine olives, olive juice, ricotta (or cottage) cheese, and eggs. Spread over top of meat mixture. Sprinkle with parmesan cheese. Bake uncovered in 375°F oven about 25 minutes until heated through. Serves 6 to 8.

Indian Meatloaf

1 pound ground venison
1 tablespoon cooking oil
16-ounce can whole kernel corn (2 cups)
1 small onion, chopped
½ teaspoon salt
¼ teaspoon celery salt or 1 stalk celery,
*   minced, plus ⅛ teaspoon salt*
Salt
2 eggs
½ cup cornmeal

Brown venison in oil. When cooked through, add onion, corn, and salts, and cook 10 minutes more. Add eggs and cornmeal and cook another 15 minutes. Put in greased loaf pan and bake 30 to 45 minutes at 350°F. Slice and serve with your favorite brown gravy. Serves 4.

Mexican Biscuit Pie

1 to 1½ pounds ground venison
1 onion, diced
4 ounces diced green chilies (½ cup)
1 teaspoon chili powder
¼ teaspoon garlic salt or 1 clove garlic,
    minced
½ teaspoon salt
⅛ teaspoon pepper
3 tablespoons ketchup
2 tablespoons taco sauce or use taco sauce
    recipe given on page 20
4 eggs
2 cups milk
1 cup biscuit mix
¾ cup grated cheddar cheese
½ cup grated jack cheese

Preheat oven to 375°F. Brown meat with onion, chilies, chili powder, garlic salt, salt, and pepper. Stir ketchup and taco sauce into meat mixture. Blend eggs, milk and biscuit mix in blender. Place meat mixture in buttered baking dish. Reserve 2 tablespoons of jack cheese and 2 tablespoons of cheddar cheese. Sprinkle the rest of the cheeses on the meat. Pour the biscuit mix on meat and cheese. Top with reserved cheese. Bake 35 to 40 minutes. Serves 4 to 6.

Venison Tostadas

1 pound ground venison
1 tablespoon cooking oil
½ cup chopped onion
1 clove garlic, minced
½ teaspoon chili powder
½ teaspoon salt
Cooking oil
6 to 10 small flour tortillas
8 ounces canned refried beans (1 cup)
3 large tomatoes, chopped
2 cups shredded lettuce
1½ cups grated cheddar cheese
1 cup picante sauce

In skillet, brown meat in oil with onion and garlic until meat is brown and onion is tender. Add chili powder and salt. In another skillet fry tortillas in hot oil approximately 30 seconds on each side, or until crisp. Drain excess oil on paper towel. Heat refried beans in a small saucepan. Assemble tostadas by placing a tortilla on a plate and layering meat, beans, tomato, lettuce and cheese on top of the tortilla. Top with picante sauce. Serve at once. Makes 6 to 10 tostadas.

Quick Italian Bake

1 pound ground venison
1 tablespoon cooking oil
1 small onion, chopped
½ pound smoked link sausage, cut into
   ½-inch chunks
16 ounces tomato sauce (2 cups)
1 cup water
½ teaspoon salt
½ teaspoon leaf basil
½ teaspoon leaf oregano
1 pound lasagna noodles
1 egg, beaten
1 cup ricotta or cottage cheese
2 ounces canned sliced ripe olives (¼ cup)
½ pound mozzarella cheese, thinly sliced

In a heavy skillet, brown venison with onion in hot oil. Stir in sausage, tomato sauce, water, salt, basil, and oregano. Simmer uncovered 20 minutes. Meanwhile, cook noodles according to package directions. Drain. Combine egg, ricotta (or cottage) cheese and olives. Place a small amount of sauce in bottom of 9×13 inch baking dish. Then layer half of the noodles, half of the ricotta mixture, half of the mozzarella slices, and half of the meat sauce. Repeat layers, using the rest of the ingredients. Bake at 375°F for 30 minutes. Let stand 10 minutes before serving. Serves 5 to 6.

Meatballs and Marinara Sauce

4 tablespoons olive oil
3 cloves garlic thinly sliced
46 ounces canned tomato juice (5¾ cups)
28 ounces canned tomato sauce (3½ cups)
½ teaspoon leaf oregano
¼ teaspoon leaf basil
⅓ teaspoon garlic salt
1 pound ground venison
½ cup dry breadcrumbs
1 egg
⅓ teaspoon leaf oregano
2 tablespoons Parmesan cheese
⅓ teaspoon parsley flakes
⅓ teaspoon garlic salt
1 tablespoon cooking oil

In Dutch oven, brown garlic slices in olive oil until very brown. Remove from heat, discard garlic, and let oil cool. Add tomato juice, tomato sauce, oregano, basil, and garlic salt to oil. Bring to a boil, reduce heat, and simmer for 2½ hours with lid slightly ajar to prevent splattering. Stir occasionally. Meanwhile, thoroughly mix ground venison, breadcrumbs, egg, oregano, Parmesan cheese, parsley flakes, and garlic salt. Form into balls and brown in oil in a large skillet, turning frequenty until balls are cooked completely through. Add the meatballs to the sauce and simmer together for at least 30 minutes more. Serve with any kind of pasta, topped with more Parmesan cheese. Serves 4 to 6.

Danish Venison Meatballs

---

1 pound ground venison
½ pound ground fresh pork
¼ cup flour
1 small onion, grated
¾ teaspoon salt
¼ teaspoon pepper
2 eggs
1 cup milk
1 to 2 tablespoons butter

In mixing bowl combine venison, pork, flour, onion, salt, and pepper. Mix well. Add eggs, one at a time, mixing very well. Add milk and mix thoroughly. Shape into balls, using 3 to 4 tablespoons meat mixture for each ball. Melt butter in skillet and fry balls, turning carefully, adding more butter as needed. Serve with red cabbage. Serves 4.

Swedish Venison Meatballs

¼ cup chopped onion
6 tablespoons butter
1 cup dry breadcrumbs
2⅔ cup milk
2 eggs, beaten
2 pounds ground venison
2 teaspoons salt
¼ teaspoon pepper
2 tablespoons flour

Sauté onion in 2 tablespoons butter in skillet. Soak breadcrumbs in ⅔ cup milk in a mixing bowl. Add eggs, ground venison, sautéed onion, salt and pepper; mix well. Form into 1-inch meatballs. Melt remaining 4 tablespoons butter in skillet and cook meatballs until brown. Remove meatballs; set aside. Stir flour into skillet and add remaining 2 cups milk. Cook, stirring constantly, until thickened. Return meatballs to gravy. Simmer 15 minutes and serve hot. Serves 6 to 8.

Spaghetti Pie

8 ounces uncooked spaghetti
3 tablespoons margarine
3 beaten eggs
½ cup grated Parmesan cheese
1⅓ cups cream style cottage cheese
1½ pounds ground venison
1 tablespoon cooking oil
½ teaspoon garlic salt
16 ounces canned tomato sauce (2 cups)
1 teaspoon leaf oregano
⅓ teaspoon leaf basil
¾ cup grated mozzarella cheese

Cook spaghetti in saucepan according to directions on package. Drain. Place in a mixing bowl and stir margarine into hot spaghetti. Stir in eggs and Parmesan cheese; mix well. Place in a greased deep-dish pie pan to form a "crust" for the pie. Spread cottage cheese over spaghetti. In skillet, brown venison in oil, adding garlic salt, until meat loses all pink color. Stir in tomato sauce, oregano, and basil. Simmer 10 minutes. Turn meat into spaghetti crust. Bake uncovered at 350°F for 20 minutes. Sprinkle with mozzarella cheese and bake 10 minutes longer. Serves 5 to 6.

Ham and Venison Crepes

½ pound ground venison
¼ teaspoon salt
1 tablespoon cooking oil
1 cup chopped ham
¼ cup flour
1 cup beef bouillon
¼ cup sliced canned mushrooms
1 tablespoon butter
1 tablespoon flour
1 cup milk
1 tablespoon Parmesan cheese
3 tablespoons grated Swiss cheese
½ teaspoon prepared mustard

Brown ground venison and salt in oil. Add chopped ham and flour and stir. Add beef bouillon and sliced mushrooms and simmer for 30 minutes. Meanwhile in a saucepan melt butter and add 1 tablespoon flour, stirring with wire whisk. Add 1 cup milk, stirring constantly over moderate heat until sauce is thickened. Add Parmesan and Swiss cheeses and prepared mustard. Fill 8 crepes with meat mixture. Roll up crepes and place in baking dish. Pour sauce over top of crepes and bake for 25 minutes at 375°F. Serves 8.

Crepe Batter

4 eggs
¼ teaspoon salt
2 cups flour
2¼ cups milk
¼ cup melted butter or oil

Combine all ingredients in a blender and blend one minute. Scrape sides of bowl with rubber spatula for another 15 seconds or until smooth. Refrigerate at least one hour and then cook in crepe pan and store until ready to use.

Venison Filled Crepes

---

3 to 3½ pounds venison roast
¼ teaspoon garlic salt
½ teaspoon salt
⅛ teaspoon pepper
1 package (1½ ounces) onion soup mix
10¾ ounces condensed cream of mushroom
    soup
1 cup dry red wine
1 cup flour
4 ounces canned sliced mushrooms (½ cup),
    or 1 cup sliced fresh mushrooms
10 to 15 cooked crepes

Sprinkle roast with salt, pepper, and garlic salt. Place in Dutch oven and add dry onion soup mix, undiluted mushroom soup, wine, and 1 cup water. Cover and simmer 4 to 4½ hours or until meat is tender. Remove meat. Dissolve flour in small amount of water and gradually stir into boiling meat broth, stirring constantly. Stir in mushrooms and remove from heat when sauce is thickened. Meanwhile slice meat thinly into pieces about ½ × 2 inches. Place 3 or 4 tablespoons meat slices on each cooked crepe and top with 1 tablespoon sauce. Place in shallow baking dish. Pour remaining sauce over filled crepes. Cover and bake 20 minutes at 350°F. Makes 10 to 15 crepes. (See preceding crepe recipe if you don't have an old family favorite.)

Swiss Venison

---

2 pounds of venison round steak
¾ cup tomato sauce
2 tablespoons cooking oil
1 teaspoon salt
1 teaspoon prepared mustard
¼ teaspoon pepper
4 ounces canned mushroom pieces
1 bay leaf, crushed
½ cup diced onion

Place meat in baking pan on a large sheet of aluminum foil. Combine remaining ingredients and pour over meat. Bring ends of foil up over meat and wrap tightly so none of the marinade can leak out. Refrigerate for 1 hour, or overnight if possible. Bake at 350°F for 1½ hours or until venison is tender. Serves 5 to 6.

Venison Style Fajitas

2 pounds thin, round venison steak
12 ounces beer
1 cup Italian oil-and-vinegar salad dressing
Sour cream
Grated cheese
Hot taco sauce/or use Taco Sauce recipe in
  Soups and Sauces section of this book
12 flour tortillas

Pierce meat with fork and place in shallow baking dish. Mix beer and Italian dressing together and pour over meat. Marinate overnight. Grill or bake steak 45 minutes or until done, basting periodically with marinade. Slice meat into thin strips. Heat tortillas in microwave, oven, or bun warmer. On a hot flour tortilla, layer thinly sliced steak, sour cream, grated cheese and hot sauce. Roll up and eat with fingers. Makes 12.

Chimichangas

2 pounds venison chunks
1½ cups water
2 cloves garlic, minced
2 tablespoons chili powder
2 tablespoons vinegar
2 teaspoons crushed leaf oregano
1 teaspoon salt
1 teaspoon ground cumin
Pepper
1 dozen large flour tortillas
Cooking oil
2 cups shredded lettuce
2 cups guacamole (recipe given on page 00)

In saucepan, combine meat, water, garlic, chili powder, vinegar, oregano, salt, cumin, and pepper. Bring to a boil. Cover; reduce heat and simmer 2 hours or until meat is very tender. Uncover and simmer 15 minutes longer or until almost all of the water has evaporated. Remove from heat and shred meat, using two forks. Heat tortillas. Spoon ¼-cup meat mixture onto each tortilla near edge. Fold edge nearest filling, up and over filling, covering the mixture. Fold up the two sides envelope fashion and roll up. Fasten with toothpicks. In skillet fry filled tortillas in hot oil until tortillas are golden brown. Drain on paper towels. Keep warm and top with lettuce and guacamole. Makes 12.

Zumbo Enchiladas

2 pounds ground venison
½ teaspoon garlic salt, or one clove
    garlic, minced, plus ¼ teaspoon salt
½ small onion, chopped
10¾ ounces condensed cream of chicken
    soup
½ cup sour cream
2 ounces canned green chilies
1 cup grated cheddar cheese
⅓ cup picante sauce
2 tablespoons grated cheddar cheese
1 dozen corn tortillas
½ cup cooking oil
½ soup can of water (5 ounces)

Brown ground meat with garlic salt and onions. Remove from heat. Mix soup, sour cream, chilies, one cup cheese, and picante sauce into meat mixture. Fry tortillas in hot oil briefly on both sides in skillet. Drain excess oil onto paper towels as you remove them from skillet. Fill each tortilla with meat mixture and place in a shallow baking dish. Top with remaining meat mixture. Add water carefully to the sides of the dish. Top with the remaining two tablespoons of cheese. Bake at 350°F for 30 minutes. Makes 12 enchiladas.

Ground Venison Enchiladas

2 tablespoons cooking oil
1½ pounds ground venison
½ teaspoon garlic salt, or 1 clove garlic, minced
    plus ¼ teaspoon salt
2 cups canned enchilada sauce or 2 cups
    enchilada sauce (recipe on page 20)
½ cup sliced olives
½ cup cooking oil
1 dozen corn tortillas
2½ cups grated cheddar cheese
1 large onion, chopped
½ cup shredded lettuce
½ cup sour cream

Brown meat in oil with garlic salt and salt. Add 4 tablespoons of enchilada sauce and cook 5 minutes to blend flavors. Add olives and stir. Set aside. Fry tortillas in skillet very briefly on both sides in ½-cup oil. Blot excess oil with paper towels. Fill tortillas with meat mixture, some grated cheese, chopped onion, and a spoonful of enchilada sauce. Roll up and place in baking dish. Pour remaining enchilada sauce over filled tortillas. Top with remaining cheese. Bake at 350°F for 30 to 35 minutes. Remove from oven and top with sour cream and shredded lettuce. Makes 12 enchiladas.

Hank's Curry

---

2 to 4 tablespoons cooking oil
1 onion, sliced
1 clove garlic, sliced very thin
1 tablespoon curry powder
1 pound venison steak, in 1-inch cubes
½ teaspoon salt
½ cup tomato paste
1 cup beef broth
1 lime or lemon

Heat oil in skillet, add onions and garlic, and cook until brown. Add curry powder; stir and continue to fry 2 to 3 minutes. Add the meat and cook on all sides. Stir in tomato paste and broth. Cover and simmer for 1½ hours, or until meat is tender and gravy thick. Add the juice from the lime or lemon. Serve over rice. Serves 4.

Quick Pizza

1 pound ground venison
½ cup quick-cooking oatmeal
½ teaspoon onion salt
¼ teaspoon garlic salt
1½ tablespoon salad oil
1 cup Marinara Sauce (see recipe on page 21)
1 cup water
1 package (8 ounces) refrigerated butterflake
  dinner rolls (12 rolls to package)
1 cup ricotta cheese
4 ounces shredded mozzarella cheese
1½ tablespoons Parmesan cheese

Preheat oven to 375°F. Lightly mix venison, oatmeal, onion salt, and garlic salt. Brown mixture in oil until completely cooked, breaking into small pieces with a fork. Add Marinara Sauce and water. Bring to a boil; reduce heat and simmer 20 minutes or until very thick. Remove dinner rolls from package and separate each roll in half to make 24 thinner rolls. Layer 12 rolls on bottom of a 9-inch pie plate. Press edges together to cover bottom. Spoon ½-cup ricotta evenly over roll layer. Top with half of cooked meat mixture. Sprinkle with ½ cup mozzarella. Repeat layers of ricotta, meat, and mozzarella. Top with remaining rolls. Bake in 375°F oven for 15 minutes. Sprinkle with Parmesan cheese; bake 5 minutes more until rolls are golden brown. Cut into wedges. Serves 4 to 6.

Venison Parmesan

1½ pounds venison round steak (¼ to ½ inch
   thick)
½ cup dry breadcrumbs
½ teaspoon leaf oregano
½ teaspoon garlic salt
½ teaspoon salt
1 egg
2 tablespoons milk
4 to 5 tablespoons olive oil
2 cups Marinara Sauce (see recipe on page 21)
½ pound mozzarella cheese, thinly sliced
Parmesan cheese

Cut meat into serving-sized pieces. Pound steaks with meat mallet until thin and flat. In small bowl, mix together breadcrumbs, oregano, garlic salt, and salt. Beat together egg and milk with fork in another bowl. Dip each piece of meat in egg and then in breadcrumb mixture until well coated with crumbs. Place pieces on waxed paper for 10 to 15 minutes; then fry in olive oil until golden brown. Spread 2 or 3 tablespoons marinara sauce in the bottom of a shallow baking dish to prevent sticking. Arrange steaks in the dish, and cover each piece of meat with slices of cheese. Top with remaining sauce and sprinkle with Parmesan cheese. Cover and bake 1 hour in 325°F oven or until meat is very tender. Serves 5.

Hawaiian Venison

1 pound venison steaks
¼ cup flour
¼ cup butter or margarine
½ cup boiling water
¼ teaspoon leaf basil
½ teaspoon rosemary
1 teaspoon salt
⅛ teaspoon pepper
2 to 3 green peppers, diced
¾ cup pineapple chunks, drained

Cut steaks into cubes. Dredge in flour and brown in Dutch oven in butter or margarine. Add water, basil, rosemary, salt, and pepper and simmer, covered, until tender, about 1 to 1 ½ hours. Add green pepper and pineapple chunks and simmer 5 minutes. Meanwhile prepare sauce recipe. Pour into Dutch oven. Bring everything to a boil, stirring constantly. Reduce heat and simmer 5 minutes. Serve over Chinese noodles or cooked rice. Serves 4 to 6.

Sauce

2½ teaspoons cornstarch
½ cup pineapple juice
¼ cup vinegar
½ cup sugar
2½ teaspoons soy sauce

Tamale Pie

---

1 pound ground venison
½ teaspoon salt
¼ teaspoon pepper
¼ cup onions, shredded
2 teaspoons chili powder
15 ounces creamed corn (2 cups)
2 cups whole tomatoes, undrained
½ cup sliced black olives
2 ounces canned green chilies, diced
⅓ cup corn meal

Sprinkle meat with salt and pepper and brown with onions. Add chili powder, corn, tomatoes, olives, and green chilies. Mix in cornmeal; continue stirring until mixture boils. Simmer 20 to 30 minutes. Serves 4.

Venison Steak Mexican Style

2 to 3 pounds venison round steak,
   2 inches thick
2 tablespoons coarse kosher-style salt
½ cup tequila
3 tablespoons lime juice
2 tablespoons olive oil
1 teaspoon freshly grated orange
   peel
1 small dried red pepper, crushed

Trim fat from meat. Rub salt into meat and place in a shallow dish. Combine tequila, lime juice, olive oil, orange peel, and pepper. Pour over meat and refrigerate 6 to 8 hours, turning every few hours. Grill meat until done over charcoal coals, basting with marinade several times.

Venison Flautas

2 cups thinly sliced strips of leftover
    venison roast
1 tablespoon cooking oil
1 tablespoon red wine vinegar
1½ teaspoon chili powder
½ teaspoon salt
½ teaspoon crumbled leaf oregano
⅛ teaspoon garlic powder, or ½ clove
    garlic, minced finely
Cooking oil
12 corn tortillas
Guacamole (recipe on page 22)

In skillet, brown meat in hot oil. Drain. Add vinegar, chili
powder, salt, oregano, and garlic powder. Toss to coat. Set
aside. Pour oil to a depth of 1 inch in saucepan. Heat. Fry each
tortilla briefly on each side just until soft but not browned
(about 5 seconds). Drain tortillas on paper toweling. Spoon
meat into tortillas. Roll up and secure with toothpicks. Fry in
hot oil in saucepan until crisp (about 2 minutes). Remove
carefully from saucepan and top with a dollop of Guacamole
Sauce. Serves 6.

Tamale Steak

2 to 2½ pounds venison round steak
½ teaspoon salt
⅛ teaspoon garlic salt
¼ teaspoon onion salt
⅛ teaspoon pepper
15 ounces canned tamales in sauce
1 teaspoon instant beef bouillon granules
½ cup boiling water
8 ounces tomato sauce
⅛ teaspoon bottled hot sauce
½ cup monterey jack or Swiss cheese, grated

Pound meat with a meat mallet on both sides. Sprinkle with salt, garlic salt, onion salt, and pepper. Unwrap tamales and place in bowl, breaking them up slightly with a fork. Spread over steaks. Roll up jelly-roll style. Tie closed with thread. Place in a shallow baking dish. In a saucepan dissolve bouillon in boiling water. Mix in tomato sauce and hot sauce. Pour over meat. Bake uncovered at 350°F for 1½ to 2 hours, or until meat is fork tender, basting with sauce often. Remove string and cut into serving-sized pieces. Top meat with cheese and serve hot. Serves 8.

Mexican Lasagna Casserole

1 to 1½ pounds ground venison
½ cup chopped green peppers
1 medium onion, chopped
1 cup fresh green chili peppers,
*   chopped, or 4 ounces canned chilies*
2 cups cottage cheese
4 ounces ripe olives
8 ounces canned green chili salsa (sauce)
½ cup grated cheddar cheese
½ cup grated monterey jack cheese
10-ounce package tortilla chips

Brown meat with peppers, onion, and chilies. In a greased baking dish, layer cottage cheese, olives, and green chili salsa. Mix cheeses and chips together, add to baking dish, and top with the meat mixture. Bake at 350°F for 20 to 30 minutes. Serve topped with guacamole (recipe given on page 22), sour cream, and cherry tomatoes. Serves 4 to 6.

South of the Border Casserole

1½ pounds ground venison
1 tablespoon cooking oil
¼ teaspoon garlic salt, or 1 clove garlic,
    minced, plus ⅛ teaspoon salt
½ teaspoon salt
1 teaspoon dried minced onion, or
    ¼ medium onion, finely grated
½ cup Taco Sauce (recipe given on page 20)
½ cup ketchup
1 dozen small corn tortillas
¾ cup grated cheddar cheese
¾ cup chopped ripe olives
½ cup water

Brown ground venison in oil in skillet. Season with garlic salt, salt, and onion, and cook until meat loses pink color. Meanwhile, mix Taco Sauce and ketchup together in a small bowl (adding more taco sauce if desired). Tear tortillas into bite-sized pieces and place on a plate. In a greased 2-quart casserole, layer meat mixture, taco sauce mixture, cheese, olives and tortillas; repeat until all ingredients are used. Top with ½-cup water. Cover and bake at 350°F for 30 to 45 minutes. Serves 4 to 6.

Deer Tacos

1 tablespoon cooking oil
1½ pounds ground venison
¼ teaspoon garlic salt
1 teaspoon instant chopped onion
½ teaspoon salt
¼ cup tomato sauce
2 tablespoons taco sauce
1 dozen crisp preformed taco shells
1½ cup grated cheddar cheese
1 cup chopped lettuce
½ cup onion, diced
2 tomatoes, diced
¾ cup bottled taco sauce, or use Taco
    Sauce recipe on page 20

Heat oil in skillet. Brown venison in skillet with garlic salt, onion, and salt. Add tomato sauce and Taco Sauce. Fill taco shells with a small amount of meat mixture, cheese, onion, lettuce, tomatoes and top with taco sauce. Serves 4 to 6.

SAUSAGE AND JERKY

Venison Pork Sausage

---

5 pounds lean venison
2 pounds salt pork
5 tablespoons dried sage
4 teaspoons salt
2 teaspoons cayenne pepper
1 onion, chopped
Juice of 1 lemon

Grind meat and salt pork together in a meat grinder to a fine consistency. Mix in remaining ingredients. Stuff into sausage casings and tie ends, or fry in patties. (This makes a large batch of sausage. If you aren't going to use it in a couple of weeks, just freeze it.)

Quick Jerky

Venison round steak
Sugar Cure (smoke flavored)
Steak sauce

Slice meat into strips being careful to trim off any fat. Rub Sugar Cure into each strip. Place strips on a rack in oven at 140 to 200°F. Leave door ajar so steam can escape. Dry to taste. After strips are dried (about 10 to 20 hours), brush steak sauce on all sides.

Oven Jerky

Venison roast
Seasoned salt
Liquid smoke

Chill or freeze meat. Slice venison across the grain as thinly as possible. Salt all pieces thoroughly with seasoned salt and brush lightly with liquid smoke. Line oven with aluminum foil to catch drippings. Drape slices of meat on oven racks so all sides are exposed to the air. Set oven at 175°F and bake meat until fat begins to drip; then reduce heat to 140°F and continue drying, with door ajar, for 6 to 7 hours.

Jerked Venison

3 pounds venison, cut into strips 6 × 2 × 1 inches
3 pounds salt
4 tablespoons allspice
5 tablespoons pepper

Use as freshly killed venison as possible. Mix salt, allspice, and pepper and rub this curing mixture on *thoroughly*. Tie a string on one end of each piece of meat and hang inside a wire-mesh box to keep insects away. Hang box in a sunny spot and let meat dry in fresh air for about 1 month. Never let the meat get wet during the drying period.

Venison Summer Sausage

4 pounds pork
12 pounds venison
3 tablespoons meat tenderizer
½ cup smoke salt
3 teaspoons pepper
1 teaspoon liquid smoke
3 tablespoons whole mustard seed

Grind pork and venison together in meat grinder. Add remaining ingredients and mix well. Cover with plastic wrap and let stand overnight in a cool place. Stuff into sausage casings. Tie shut and let stand in cool place overnight. Smoke for about 4 hours, and leave sausage in smoker overnight. Then smoke another 4 hours or to taste. Let stand overnight again. Keep refrigerated until served. Note: For best results, this recipe should be prepared in the winter.

Deer Sausage with Mint

1¾ pounds ground venison
1¾ pounds ground pork
1 tablespoon salt
1 teaspoon red cayenne pepper
⅛ teaspoon garlic powder
1 teaspoon cumin
1 teaspoon poultry seasoning
⅛ teaspoon sage
⅛ teaspoon curry powder
1 teaspoon dried mint, or 5 leaves
    fresh mint, minced

Grind the venison and pork together and mix well. Then mix in the rest of the ingredients. Form into patties and fry 'em up.

Easy Salami

4 pounds ground venison
½ pound ground beef suet
2 teaspoons black pepper
½ teaspoon onion salt
1½ teaspoons garlic powder
5 teaspoons salt
2½ teaspoons liquid smoke
1½ teaspoons small red chilies

Mix all ingredients in a non-metal bowl. Refrigerate for 3 days, thoroughly mixing each day with hands. On the fourth day divide mixture into 5 parts. Knead and form into long thin logs, about 12 inches long. Place logs on cookie sheet and bake at 155°F. After 5 hours, turn logs over and cook 5 hours more. Remove from oven and roll in paper towels to remove excess grease. Cool, wrap in foil and keep in refrigerator. Makes five 12-inch logs.

Speedy Sausage

2 pounds ground venison
1 teaspoon garlic salt
½ teaspoon onion salt
1 tablespoon liquid smoke
2 tablespoons sesame seeds
3 tablespoons curing salt

Place all ingredients in a bowl and mix well. Wrap in aluminum foil in a log shape and bake at 350°F for 1¼ to 1½ hours.

Charcoal-Grill Jerky

Venison strips
1 gallon water
½ pound salt
Sugar
Caraway seed
Curry powder

Cut venison into strips 1 to 1½ inches wide and about 5 inches long. Mix water and salt in a stone crock or plastic bucket. Add meat. Weight it so liquid covers the entire surface of it. Brine meat for 24 to 36 hours. Remove the meat and rinse with fresh water. Sprinkle sugar moderately on meat. Place meat on broiler tray. Make a mixture of 1 part caraway seed (browned in oven and ground) to 2 parts curry powder. Sprinkle on meat and broil about 10 inches from heat in oven for 20 to 30 minutes. Remove meat and smoke in a covered charcoal grill as follows: Place a small pile of charcoal briquets in one corner of grill and light. Soak hickory chips in water for 30 minutes and then place on charcoal after it is burning well. Arrange chips so they cover charcoal completely. Place venison strips on the far corner of grill. Lower lid and smoke for 2 to 3 hours, keeping top and bottom vents open. Store jerky in airtight container.

OTHER IDEAS FOR VENISON

Canned Venison

4 pounds venison roast
Salt
Water

Roast venison at 350°F for 15 minutes per pound of meat. Slice into pieces about ¾ inch thick and about 2 inches square. Pack into sterilized fruit jars to within 1 inch of rim. Add 1 teaspoon of salt to quart jars and ½ teaspoon salt to pint jars. Add 3 tablespoons water to each jar. Wipe rim with clean towel. Put on cap, screw band firmly tight. Process in a pressure cooker: pints for 75 minutes and quarts for 90 minutes at 10 pounds pressure. Follow manufacturer's directions for operation of your particular pressure cooker. Do *not* process in a water bath.

Deer Spread

Cooked slices of venison roast
Bread and butter pickles
Dill pickles
Salt
Pepper
Garlic salt
Mayonnaise
Brown spicy prepared mustard

Grind leftover meat with pickles in meat grinder. Add seasonings to taste and enough mayonnaise to make mixture a spreadable consistency. Add mustard and mix well. Makes a great sandwich filling or spread for crackers.

Crescent Hors d'oeuvres

2 tablespoons cooking oil
1 pound ground venison
½ teaspoon dried minced onion
¼ teaspoon celery salt
¼ teaspoon garlic salt
¼ teaspoon salt
⅛ teaspoon pepper
¼ teaspoon paprika
1 tablespoon soy sauce
30 unbaked refrigerated crescent rolls

Preheat oven to 400°F. Heat oil in skillet and brown venison with dried seasonings until all the meat is cooked through. Stir in soy sauce. Unroll preshaped crescent dough and roll out into flat triangles. Place 1 to 2 teaspoons of meat mixture in the center of each triangle. Roll up carefully and place on greased baking sheet. Bake for 10 to 15 minutes or until crescents are golden brown.

Venison Chili Salad

1 head iceberg lettuce
3 cups corn chips
2 tomatoes, diced
1 cup shredded cheddar cheese
15 ounces ripe black olives, drained
2 cups Western Chili from recipe found
   on page 30

Cut lettuce into chunks in salad bowl. Add tomatoes, cheese, olives, and chips. Warm chili. Toss salad with chili.

Trailside Delight

Jerky
Unsalted, roasted peanuts
Raisins
Sunflower seeds
M & M candy-coated chocolate candies
Dried bananas

Use your favorite jerky recipe. Cut jerky into small bits and add equal portions of other ingredients. Put a handful or two into your backpack or lunchpail to keep you going in any situation.

Chislic

---

2 pounds venison, cut into ½-inch cubes
1 cup cooking oil
½ teaspoon salt
⅛ teaspoon pepper
¼ teaspoon garlic salt
¼ teaspoon onion salt

Fry meat in deep fat until tender. Sprinkle salt, pepper, garlic and onion salts on meat and serve with Barbecue Sauce (recipe on page 19) and crackers.

Venison Nibbles

1½ pounds venison steak
¼ to ½ teaspoon salt
¼ teaspoon pepper
1 egg
½ teaspoon minced onion flakes
Cracker crumbs

Cut venison into 1 × 3 inch strips. Beat egg with onion flakes. Dip meat strips in egg mixture and then in cracker crumbs. Deep fry in hot oil until golden brown. Makes excellent family snacks or hors d'oeuvres.

Peachy Venison Salad

1½ cups cooked venison roast, diced
4 cups romaine lettuce, torn into bite-
    sized pieces
3 cups fresh spinach, torn into bite-sized
    pieces
3 fresh medium peaches, peeled, pitted,
    and sliced
1 ripe avocado, peeled, pitted, and
    sliced
12 cherry tomatoes, halved
½ cup salad oil
3 tablespoons vinegar
1 teaspoon prepared horseradish
½ teaspoon salt
½ teaspoon Worcestershire sauce
⅛ teaspoon pepper
2 drops bottled hot pepper sauce

In salad bowl, combine cooked venison, romaine, spinach, sliced peaches, sliced avocado, and cherry tomato halves. In a small jar combine salad oil, vinegar, horseradish, salt, Worcestershire sauce, pepper, and hot pepper sauce. Cover and shake well. Just before serving, pour dressing mixture over salad and toss lightly. Serves 6 to 8.

Smothered Venison Ribs with Onion Gravy

3 to 4 pounds venison ribs, individually cut
3 tablespoons cooking oil
1 teaspoon salt
⅛ teaspoon pepper
3 medium onions, sliced
¾ cup water
2 tablespoons sugar
3 tablespoons flour
2 tablespoons vinegar

In Dutch oven, sprinkle ribs with salt and pepper and brown well in oil. Add one of the sliced onions and the water. Cover and simmer 2 to 3 hours or until meat is tender. Add additional water if needed. Transfer ribs to platter. Add water enough to make two cups of liquid. Set aside. Return three tablespoons liquid to Dutch oven. Add sugar to liquid and cook for 1 minute. Add remaining two sliced onions, and continue cooking and stirring until onion is tender. Blend in flour. Stir in reserved pan juices and cook until thickened. Return ribs to gravy until heated through; serve ribs and gravy with rice. Serves 4 to 6.

Smoky Ribs

---

4 pounds venison ribs
1 to 2 teaspoons salt (or to taste)

Sprinkle 2 teaspoons salt evenly over ribs. Start charcoal in barbecue/smoker. When coals are burning well cover them completely with hickory chips that have been soaked in water for a half hour. Place ribs, bone side down, on grill of smoker, away from coals. Close hood on smoker and cook slowly for 3½ to 4 hours, basting with Cowboy Sauce frequently. Serves 4 to 5.

Cowboy Sauce

---

1 tablespoon Worcestershire sauce
⅛ teaspoon Tabasco sauce
1 cup ketchup
1 cup water
¼ cup vinegar
1 tablespoon sugar
1 teaspoon salt
1 teaspoon sesame seed
1 teaspoon celery seed

Combine all ingredients and brush on ribs.

Tasty Venison Ribs

---

4 pounds venison ribs
⅓ cup soy sauce
½ cup pink chablis
½ teaspoon garlic salt
3½ tablespoons brown sugar
½ cup water

Place ribs in large roasting pan. Combine remaining ingredients and pour over ribs. Cover. Bake 45 minutes in 350°F oven, turning ribs several times. Remove lid and continue cooking until golden brown and well done (turning periodically). Add more water to sauce if necessary to keep ribs from sticking. Baste with sauce periodically throughout entire cooking time. Serves 4 to 5.

Venison Heart with Rice

---

1 venison heart
2 tablespoons cooking oil
1½ cups water
⅔ cup uncooked rice
⅓ cup chopped celery
¼ cup chopped green pepper
2 ounces canned mushrooms,
*   sliced*
10¾ ounces condensed cream of
*   mushroom soup*
2 tablespoons dry onion soup mix
¼ teaspoon garlic salt

Rinse heart and remove outer membrane. Cut the heart open and cube tender fleshy parts of heart, discarding gristle and venous hard parts and any fat. Brown cubes in cooking oil. Add water and simmer 45 minutes. Add uncooked rice, celery, and green pepper; bring to boil. Reduce heat; cover and simmer until rice is tender (about 20 minutes). Drain mushrooms; stir into heart mixture with mushrooms and onion soup. Simmer 10 minutes more. Serves 6.

Mexican-Style Liver

6 slices bacon
⅔ cup chopped onion
2 cloves garlic, minced
¼ cup flour
1¼ teaspoons chili powder
¾ teaspoon salt
2 ounces canned chopped green chilies
1½ pound venison liver
16 ounces or 2 cups canned whole tomatoes,
 cut up
12 ounces or 1½ cups canned whole kernel
 corn, drained
12 flour tortillas

In skillet, cook bacon until crisp. Remove bacon; crumble and set aside. Cook onion and garlic in bacon fat until onion is tender but not brown, about 5 minutes. Combine flour, chili powder and salt. Cut liver into thin strips and dredge in flour mixture. Add liver to onion in skillet and brown quickly on all sides. Stir in crumbled bacon, undrained tomatoes, chilies, and corn. Simmer covered for 15 minutes. Serve with tortillas. Serves 6.

Supper Salad

⅓ cup mayonnaise
¼ cup chili sauce (recipe given on
    page 19)
1 tablespoon sweet pickle relish
½ teaspoon salt
8 ounces canned kidney beans, drained
2 cups cooked venison roast, diced
1 cup chopped celery
½ cup chopped onion
4 eggs, hard boiled, peeled, and
    chopped

Blend together mayonnaise, chili sauce, sweet pickle relish, and salt in a jar. Combine beans, meat, celery, onion, and eggs in a mixing bowl. Add mayonnaise mixture to bowl and mix. Cover and refrigerate up to 24 hours. Stir salad just before serving. Serves 4 to 5.

Buttered Venison

2 pounds venison steaks or strips
½ teaspoon garlic salt
3 tablespoons cooking oil

When meat is partially thawed, cut meat into strips as thin as possible. Then rub with oil and sprinkle with garlic salt. Broil, turning every 30 seconds or so to sear meat. Continue cooking until the desired state of doneness is achieved. Then spread butter paste on each slice. Serve immediately as hors d'oeuvres. Serves 6.

Butter Paste

¼ cup soft butter
½ teaspoon salt
½ teaspoon pepper
1 tablespoon chopped parsley
1½ tablespoons lemon juice

Blend salt, pepper, and parsley into butter. Gradually add lemon juice.

Liver Patties

---

1 pound venison liver, diced
Boiling water
1 medium onion, sliced
10 saltine crackers
2 eggs
2 teaspoons milk
¾ teaspoon salt
¼ teaspoon pepper
Cooking oil

Place liver in a bowl and cover with boiling water. Let stand for 10 minutes. Put liver, onions, and crackers through a grinder. Place ground ingredients in a bowl and add slightly beaten eggs, milk, salt, and pepper. Heat oil in skillet and drop spoonfuls of liver mixture into oil. Flatten with spatula and fry each side until crispy brown. Serves 4 to 5.

Zee's Mincemeat

---

2 pounds venison neck pieces (boneless)
1 pound beef suet
4 pounds tart apples, peeled and quartered
4 cups sugar
2 pounds red currants
3 pounds seedless raisins
½ pound citron, finely chopped
Juice and grated peel of 3 oranges
2 cups apple juice
1 tablespoon salt
1¼ teaspoons nutmeg
½ teaspoon cinnamon

In a Dutch oven simmer venison in enough water to cover, for about 3 hours or until meat is tender. Cool; put through meat grinder with suet and apples. Return to Dutch oven and add other ingredients; mix. Simmer 1 hour. Make into pies using your favorite pastry recipe or the one given on page 128 with Venison Meat Pie, using 2 cups filling per 8-inch pie. Makes enough filling for 3 to 4 pies.

Venison Barbecue Sandwiches

2 cups cooked venison, cubed
12-ounces bottled chili sauce or 1½ cups
    homemade chili sauce (recipe given
    on page 19)
8 ounces canned tomato sauce
1 slice onion
2 tablespoons chopped green pepper
1 tablespoon Worcestershire sauce
1½ teaspoons prepared mustard
¼ teaspoon salt
½ teaspoon picante sauce (optional)
6 hamburger buns

Blend half of meat in blender until coarsely chopped and repeat with other half. Place all the chopped venison in a saucepan. In blender, combine chili sauce, tomato sauce, onion, green pepper, Worcestershire sauce, mustard, salt, and picante sauce. Cover and blend until vegetables are chopped. Stir into meat; simmer, covered, 15 to 20 minutes. Spoon ¼ cup on each bun. Serves 6.

Venison Liver and Bacon

2 pounds young deer liver, sliced ½ inch
    thick
Milk
½ cup flour
¾ teaspoon salt
½ teaspoon parsley flakes, or 1 teaspoon
    finely minced fresh parsley
½ teaspoon pepper
½ cup margarine
8 slices bacon

Refrigerate liver slices overnight in milk. Drain. Pat dry and dredge slices in mixture of flour, salt, pepper, and parsley. Saute slices in margarine over high heat until lightly brown, about five minutes on each side. In another skillet fry bacon slices until crisp. Drain bacon and serve on top of liver slices. Serves 3 to 4.

Cold Sandwich Spread

---

2 cups leftover roast venison,
    coarsely chopped
¼ cup chopped dill pickle
½ cup mayonnaise
3 tablespoons grated onion
½ cup finely cubed cheddar
    cheese
1 teaspoon prepared
    mustard

Mix all ingredients together and spread on fresh Italian bread for a delightful lunch.

Liver and Onions

---

1 small liver from a freshly killed deer
¼ teaspoon salt
⅛ teaspoon pepper
¼ cup butter or margarine
2 medium onions, sliced thin

Slice liver and skin the slices, removing the veins and cutting the liver into strips 1½ by ½ inches wide. Sprinkle liver with salt and pepper. Heat butter in a heavy skillet. Add onions and meat. Brown, stirring frequently, for 5 to 10 minutes. Cover slices and cook for 15 minutes longer, or until thoroughly done. Serves 2.

Index of Recipes